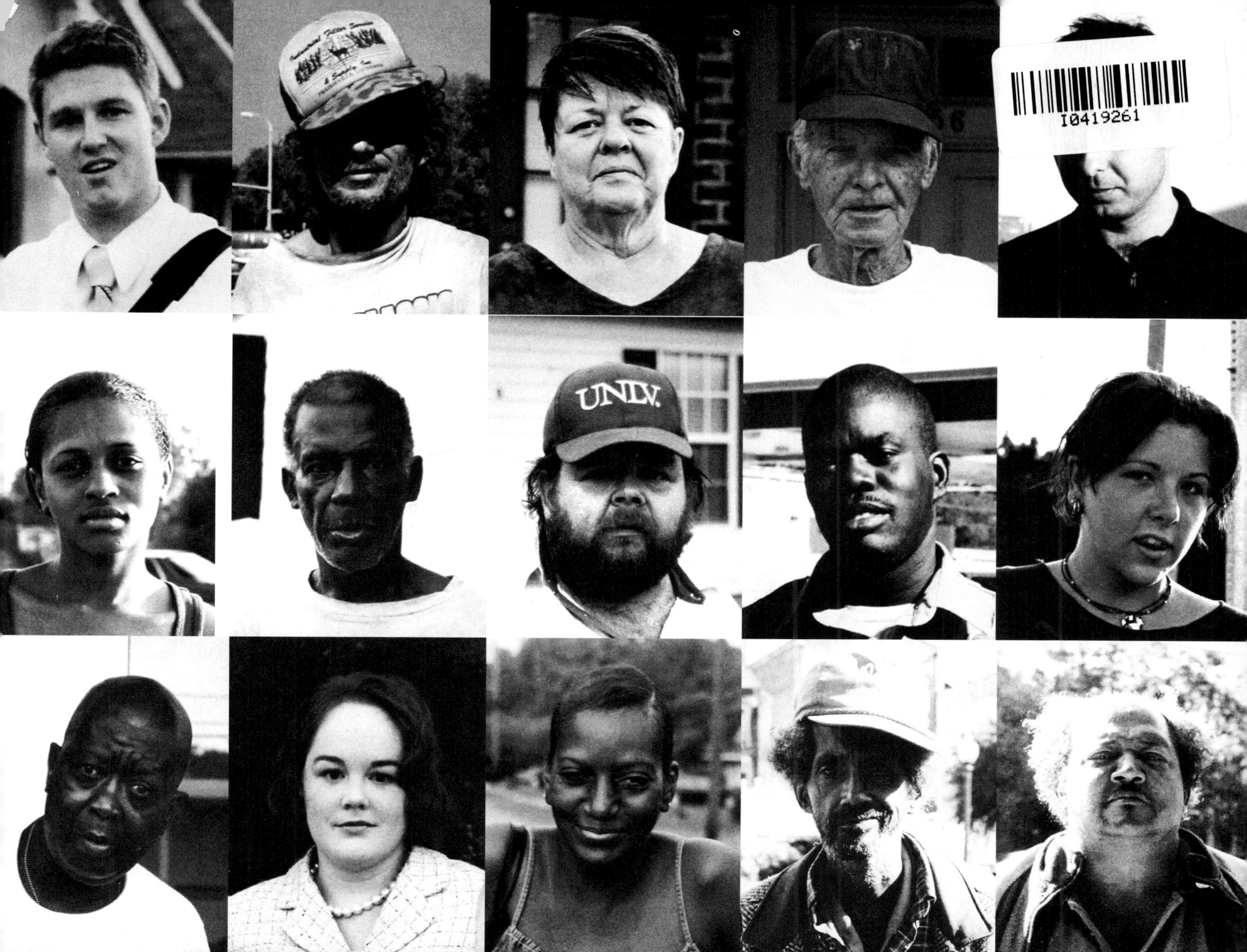

DEAD
LOST
TERRENCE
SANDERS
OR
DISPLACED

ISBN 10: 1-60801-007-4
ISBN 13: 978-1-60801-007-3

Printed in China

Designed by Britt Benoit
Collages by Terrence Sanders with assistance by Caitlin Owens

First UNO Press trade paperback edition September 2011

Quotes on pages 12-72 from The Times Picayune article,
"Peace Among The Ruins" by Chris Rose, February 03, 2006

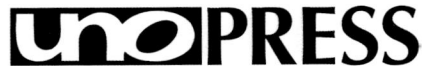

University of New Orleans Publishing
http://unopress.uno.edu

This book is dedicated to my son Lucien Smith and my mother Valerie Bryant.

Raw Juxtapositions

Shantrelle P. Lewis
Director of Programs & Exhibitions, Caribbean Cultural Center African Diaspora
Institute and former Executive Director & Curator The George & Leah McKenna Museum
of African American Art

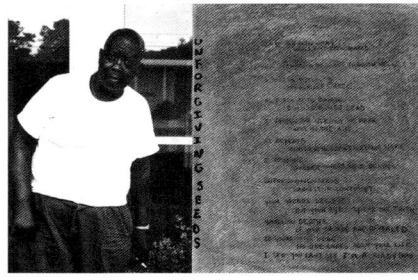 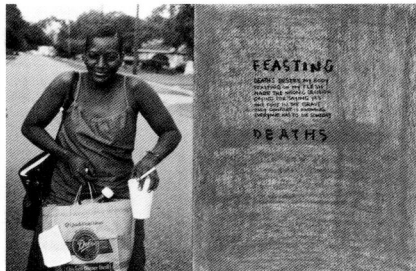 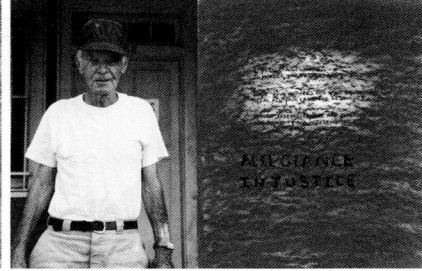

When Terrence Sanders and I first discussed the idea of exhibiting his *Dead, Lost or Displaced* Series at the George & Leah McKenna Museum of African American Art, I was resistant. "Not Katrina again" was my initial retort. "Not Katrina again" was my initial retort. As a curator in New Orleans, as a *native* of New Orleans, I had already taken my position on museums and galleries in the city showing Katrina related work. My sentiment didn't come from a place of insensitivity on my part nor did it come from a place of disrespect. It actually comes from a space much deeper, much more sensitive, much too close to the issue. The 9th ward isn't some new hip, cliché place that just recently found its way in my current conversations or travels, like it has for many post-Katrina artists and gallery owners. I'm not only from New Orleans but, my paternal family lived and had homes in the lower 9th ward. This matter is too close to home...to close to the post-traumatic stress I am helping my family to work through. But when I looked at the series, I knew it was the exception to my no Katrina rule.

Dead, Lost, or Displaced is a series of thirty-three mixed media juxtapositions – black and white; text and photograph; pairs of words and paragraphs. The works were completed during two realms of time, B.K. and P.K. (Before Katrina and Post-Katrina). Terrence traveled the streets and roads of New Orleans and Baton Rouge, capturing the essence of the people who lived in these southern landscapes and roamed there. All of the people in these pieces were photographed pre-Katrina.

In order to truly grasp the depth of this series, it's necessary for one to examine the significance of the chronological juxtaposition of a pre and post-Katrina reality. The black and white photographs, of Black and White people speak to a society that as much as it is multi-cultural, with a caste system of Black, white and something in-between, has like most Southern places, been racially bipolar. Terrence takes black and white images of Black and White people, and creates a mixed media of dry and oil pastel, graphite jambalaya. Black and White people lost their homes and lives in the storm. Black and White people had join their respective manpower, wading through the water, for survival. Yet, a disproportionate number of African Americans lost lives, homes, and have yet been able to return.

The black and white subjects/people, whose identities are

unknown pre-Katrina, become mysterious conundrums post-Katrina. What happened to them? Could they afford to evacuate or did they choose to "ride the storm out?" Terrence addresses this dilemma in "Feasting Deaths." Sanders says, "It never occurred to me that this series would become my memorial so to speak to the innocent, who either are dead, lost or displaced due to the events that occurred after Hurricane Katrina struck New Orleans." The subject, a Black woman, holds a grocery bag. Many people couldn't leave during the storm while some just simply chose to stock up on non-perishable food items and stay. What was the result of their decision, Sanders asks. Were their bodies decomposed in the flood water? Were they shuttled to another state or have they made it back home? Their existence is unknown and is representative of thousands of people who because of Katrina, and governmental politics, are now missing, dead, or living in faraway places with no way or right to return home.

The artist uses this series to give voice to the voiceless... transforming himself into what Mbiti knows to be a spirit medium, "people who get in touch with the spirit world... During their possession, they speak in a different voice... which they do not otherwise know."[1] It is during the eleven days following the aftermath of the storm, that Terrence goes back to this series and adds text, as a form of self-medication and therapy. He says, "the one thing that helped me cope was working on the words to place with the images. I began to look into the souls of my subjects, discovered their inner most fears and documented their confessions to the camera."[2] As artist/medium, Sanders captures the psyche and souls of the people that he photographed pre-Katrina, not knowing their fate, whether or not those people are dead or alive. The raw, chalky text combined with the gritty black and white portraits, adds a haunting, powerful depth to the series.

In "Unforgiving Seeds" Sanders deals with matters regarding racial divide in the deep South. Charged slurs are thrown between some unknown White stranger and this somewhat known Black man. Deeply planted seeds are clearly unforgiving and perhaps, too deeply sown to be uprooted. I remember cringing when I heard stories about unarmed African Americans being murdered by racist vigilantes in days directly following Katrina. In Louisiana, on any given day, one will see Confederate flags waving proudly in the sky, or bumper stickers with this same symbol donned on

the back of a pick-up trucks. Despite what many utopian romanticists say about a post-racial society, Obama's election does not mark a time when racial tensions do not exist. In Louisiana and other places around the country, "Unforgiving Seeds harvest in contempt. Your words deceive but your eyes speak the truth. Shallow depths of your façade are revealed."[3]

Robert Alan Asistent states "Terrence's images are a direct transference from the soul of an artist to the psyche of our human nature. We are a lost people on this ship, searching for how to go beyond ego's reign of war and how instead to reach out and care for each other. This body of work is symbolic of the human tragedy that manifests in our separation instead of our integration. *Dead, Lost and Displaced* is the story we need to digest before we will ever discover: Alive, Found and Ingratiated."

Another striking piece in this series is "Allegiance Injustice." Here we have an elderly white man, wearing a worn out baseball cap, with a clean white tee shirt, tucked neatly into khaki pants held up nicely by a plain black belt. His casual wear and sense of order gives the viewer a sense of military discipline. So it's not surprising that Sanders addresses allegiance to a country, perhaps as a veteran of one of any of the 20th century wars with foreign lands. The artist goes further and deals with the issue of what happens when one's country, shows a lack of regard for his long term faith and service. Also questioned is the moral decision or lack thereof that one makes when placed in a war situation. What sentiments are evoked when one fights people over resources and land, only because of a patriotic duty to serve the United States of America or in some cases, merely because of good benefits and a college education? Sanders' post-Katrina text is also infused with the artist's own questions about the lack of regard that was shown for America's own citizens via the tragically slow response of the government to provide help after the levees broke. We are confronted with our own level of allegiance and the levels of injustice we promote, condone or suffer from on a regular basis.

Terrence Sanders is an aggressive businessman. He's a hustler. He's a magician, having the unique talent to create a magazine, produce powerful art, or open galleries in a space when these things did not previously exist. Terrence Sanders is a brilliant artist, he finds fault with society and

intellectualizes it via his photography and mixed media productions. Utilizing text in most of his work, Sanders' pieces are the intersection where Dada meets Richard Wright meets the people parading down the interstate on N. Claiborne Avenue[4]. As both a human and humanitarian, Sanders is concerned about those whose voices are murmured in a cacophony of sound. It's no wonder his contemporary art publication, *ArtVoices*, has done so well with the established and emerging groups alike. *Dead, Lost or Displaced* gives Sanders his own voice, one that was temporarily mute as a result of immense post-traumatic shock anyone surviving Katrina has had to endure.

We hung *Dead, Lost or Displaced* alongside of much larger mixed media pieces by Sanders as part of the *Behind the Façade* show, which exhibited at the McKenna Museum during November of 2008. It was very intentional that this show coincided with the grandiose international, contemporary art world's inaugural Prospect 1. We couldn't have selected a better time or a better series to feature in the museum to accompany Malick Sidibe and Xavier Veilhan. The droves of international and national visitors were greeted with the aesthetically pleasing work of our Prospect 1 artists, yet confronted with raw realities about the true condition of New Orleans, a deeper story behind Katrina's aftermath, and the "rebuilding" effort. I vividly remember the multi-varied looks of shock and compassion on people's face during a private tour given to board members of ArtTable, as Terrence retold the stories that led to the text he incorporated into his *Dead, Lost, or Displaced* pieces. It was a hard story to listen to...an even harder story to tell. However, in a very honest and vulnerable way, Sanders shares this story through this series, with anyone who is interested enough, or brave enough to listen.

1. John Mbiti. Introduction to African Religion.Oxford, 1991 2nd. Ed., pg. 158
2. Artist statement
3. Text in "Unforgiving Seeds"
4. North Claiborne is a major avenue in New Orleans where many traditional second lines and Mardi Gras Indian processions take place. It has been a historical thoroughfare.

THE BAR IS CLOSING

Last dance, bar is closing.
Water's up to her neck,
how much longer can she hold on?
Afraid to fall asleep,
doesn't know where she'll wake up.
She lived a simple life,
consumed by bad decisions.
Listening to Satchmo,
sipping on air.
Falling deeper,
drifting under lucid spell.
She can't go any further;
her will to survive is diminishing.
One day she'll forgive them,
wishing it all could go back,
to the way it was.

Introduction

I conceptualized and created this series to document the lives of
Louisiana natives mostly in and around New Orleans and Baton Rouge.
It never occurred to me that this series would become my memorial so
to speak to the innocent, who either are dead, lost or displaced due
to the events that occurred after Hurricane Katrina struck New Orleans. During the first 11 days spent in New Orleans during the aftermath of Katrina, the one thing that helped me cope was working on
the words to place with the images. I began to look into the souls of
my subjects, discovered their inner most fears and documented their
confessions to the camera."

Terrence Sanders
New Orleans, April 3, 2009

Then I ran into Terrence Sanders,

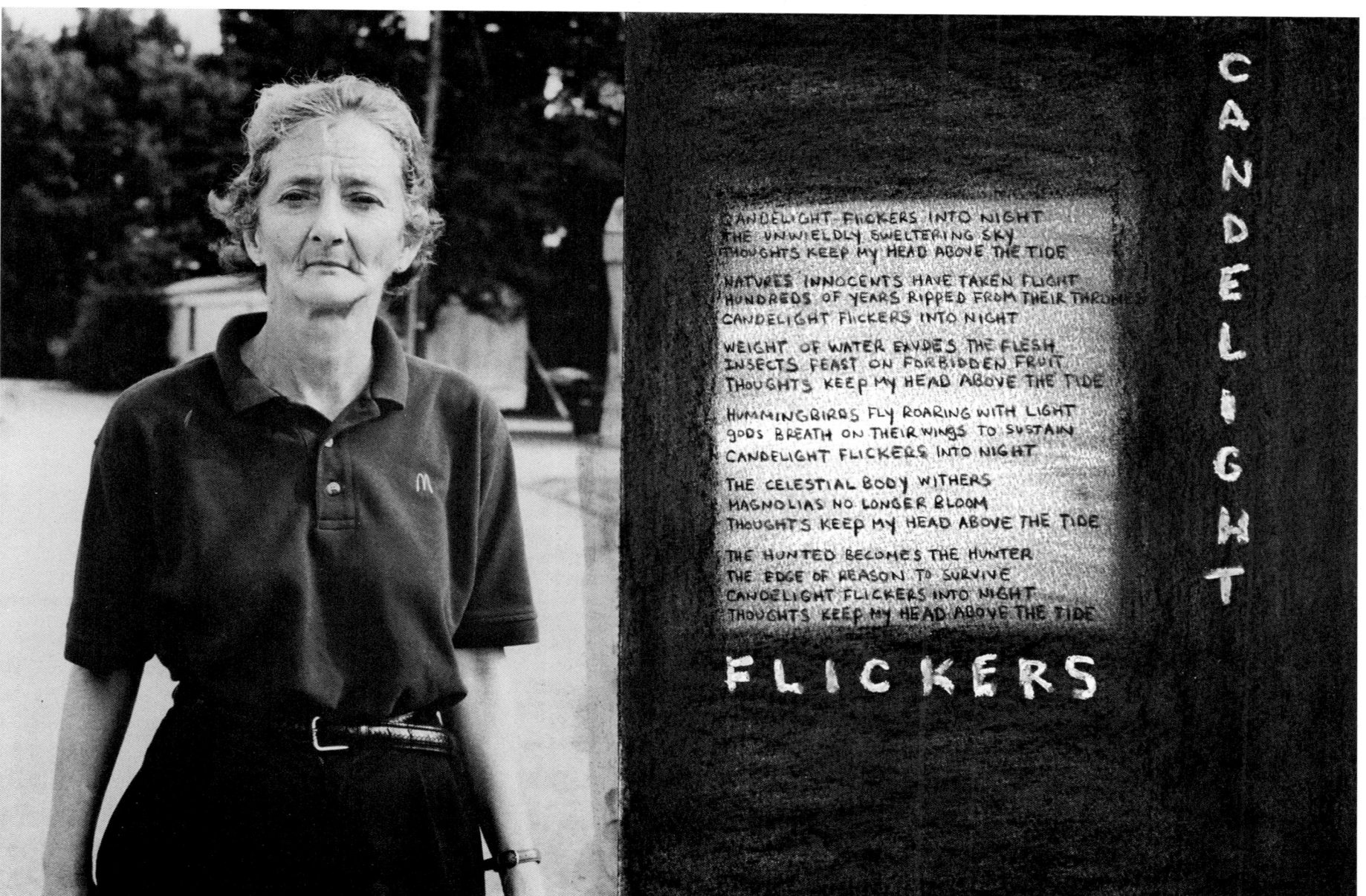

CANDELIGHT

CANDELIGHT FLICKERS INTO NIGHT
THE UNWIELDLY SWELTERING SKY
THOUGHTS KEEP MY HEAD ABOVE THE TIDE

NATURES INNOCENTS HAVE TAKEN FLIGHT
HUNDREDS OF YEARS RIPPED FROM THEIR THRONES
CANDELIGHT FLICKERS INTO NIGHT

WEIGHT OF WATER EXUDES THE FLESH
INSECTS FEAST ON FORBIDDEN FRUIT
THOUGHTS KEEP MY HEAD ABOVE THE TIDE

HUMMINGBIRDS FLY ROARING WITH LIGHT
GODS BREATH ON THEIR WINGS TO SUSTAIN
CANDELIGHT FLICKERS INTO NIGHT

THE CELESTIAL BODY WITHERS
MAGNOLIAS NO LONGER BLOOM
THOUGHTS KEEP MY HEAD ABOVE THE TIDE

THE HUNTED BECOMES THE HUNTER
THE EDGE OF REASON TO SURVIVE
CANDELIGHT FLICKERS INTO NIGHT
THOUGHTS KEEP MY HEAD ABOVE THE TIDE

FLICKERS

13

and he was the first to smooth out the mental rumples in my head,

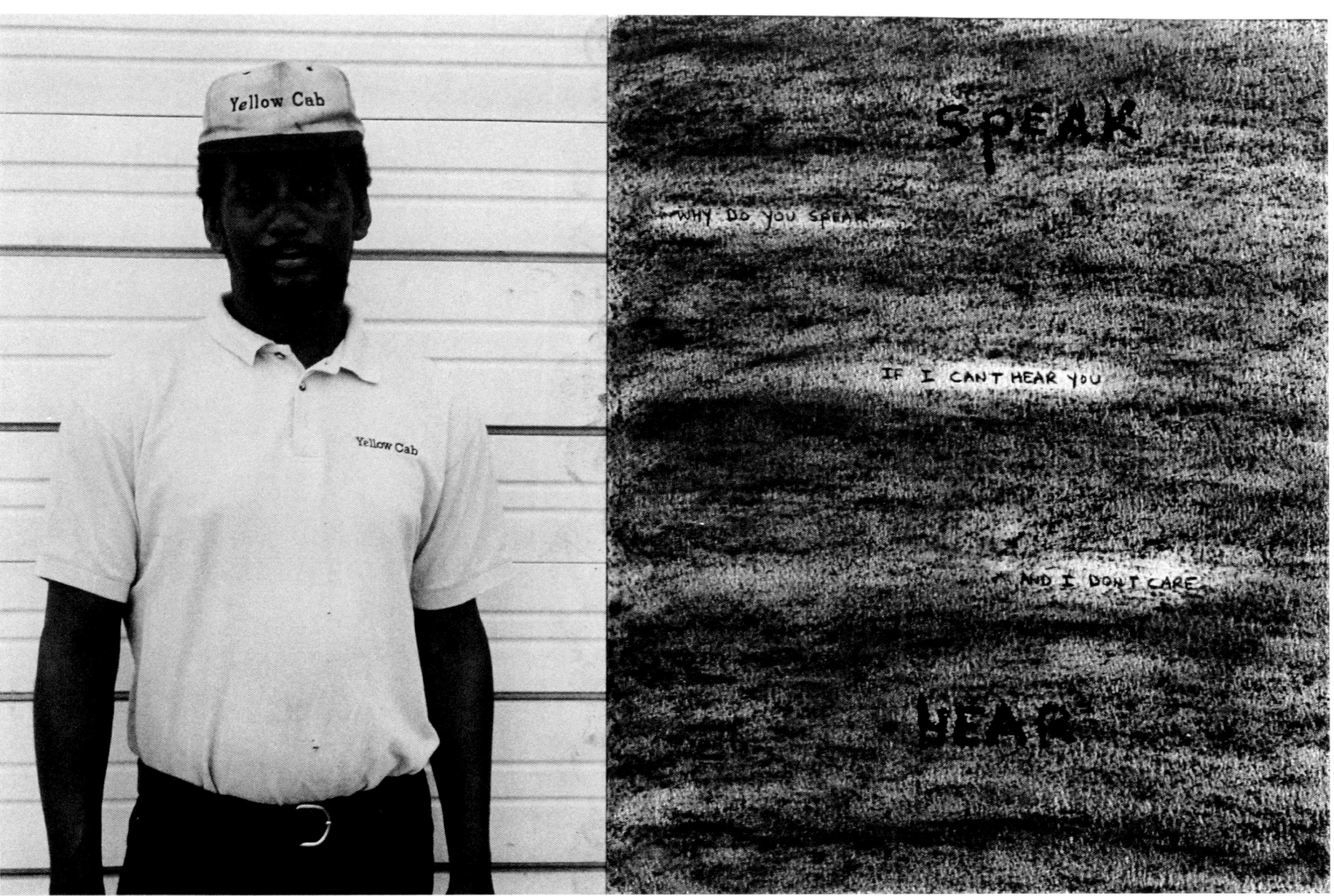

to make me feel -- even on that first day back, a time when New Or-

leans still smelled of death and rot and panic

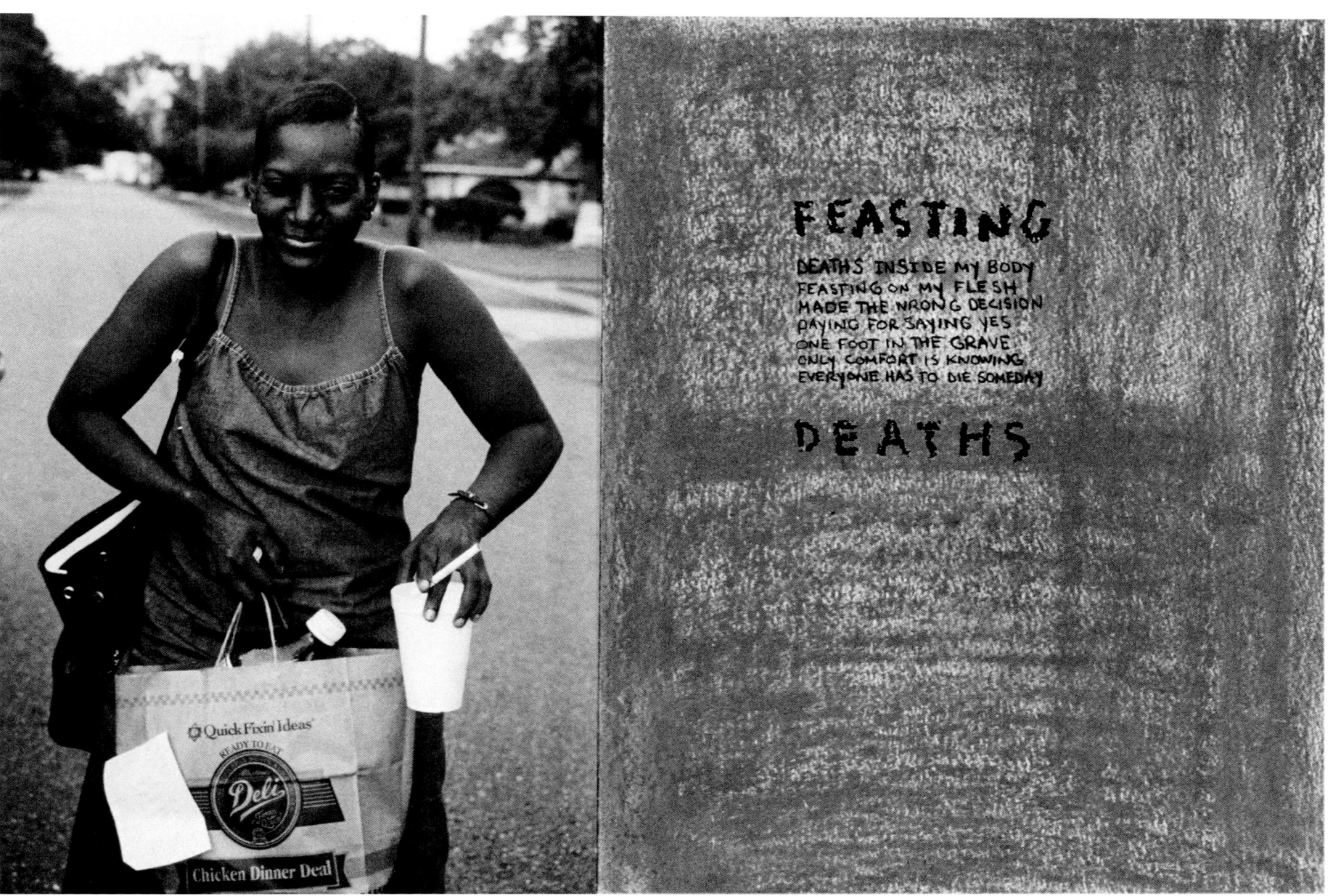

FEASTING

DEATHS INSIDE MY BODY
FEASTING ON MY FLESH
MADE THE WRONG DECISION
PAYING FOR SAYING YES
ONE FOOT IN THE GRAVE
ONLY COMFORT IS KNOWING
EVERYONE HAS TO DIE SOMEDAY

DEATHS

that one has many choices to make in life and one of those choices is simply to carry on.

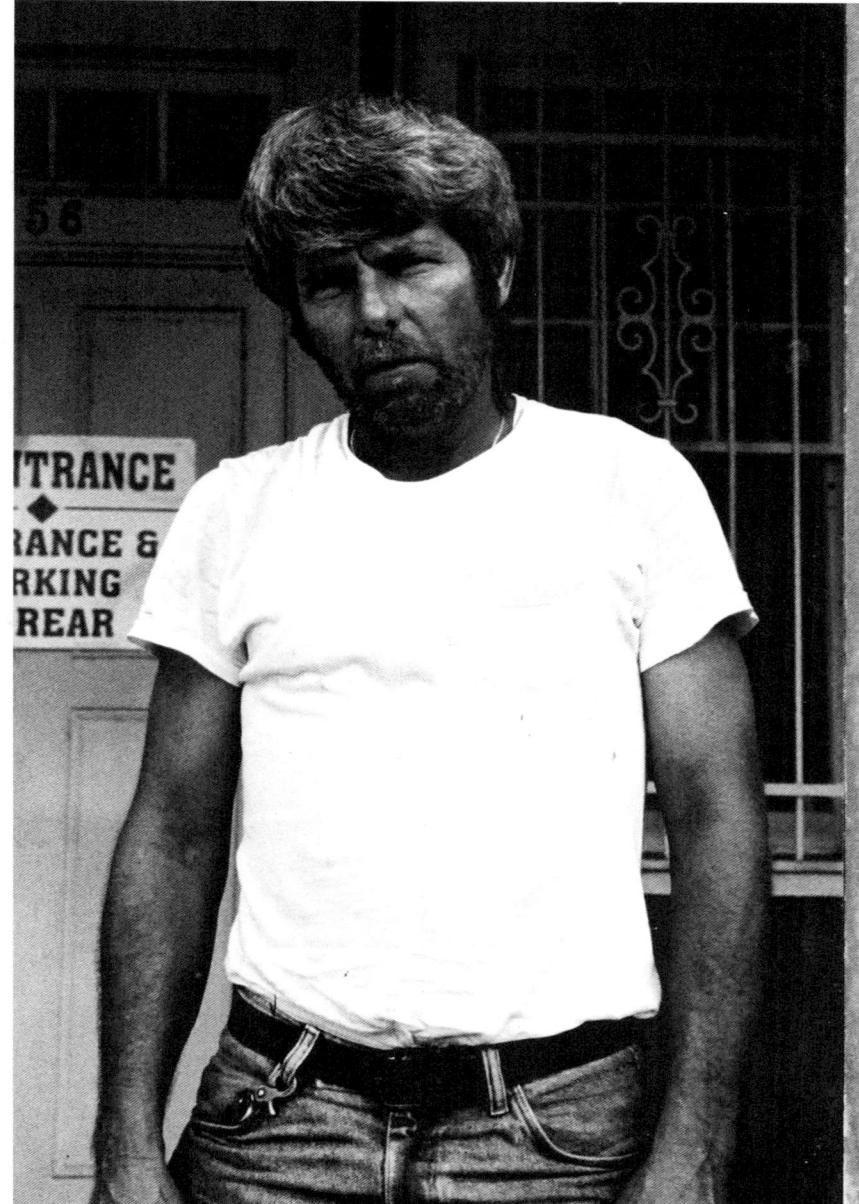

AND MISTAKES BEEN MADE DUES NOT PAID
  CONTEMPLATING WAYS TO ESCAPE
NOTHING TO SAY HASN'T BEEN SAID

MANS WORTHLESS LEECH BREAKS HIS SILENCE
  A DISGRACED WASTE OF HUMAN LIFE
AND MISTAKES BEEN MADE DUES NOT PAID

MAN IN MIRROR IS TO BLAME
  SUSPECTS AND VICTIMS APPEAR ON STAGE
NOTHING TO SAY HASN'T BEEN SAID

IN OBSCURED JADED SECLUSION
  A CLUCKING FOOLS SOULESS PARADE
AND MISTAKES BEEN MADE DUES NOT PAID

ACCUSED WALK THE LINE CLOSE TO GOD
  A HOPELESS WRETCH SENTENCED TO DEATH
NOTHING TO SAY HASN'T BEEN SAID

HIDDEN SHADOWS OF PRIDE AND SHAME
  IN DEPTHS OF HUMILITIES RAGE

AND MISTAKES BEEN MADE DUES NOT PAID
NOTHING TO SAY HASN'T BEEN SAID

NOTHING
MISTAKES

A New Orleans credo: When life gives you lemons -- make daiquiris.

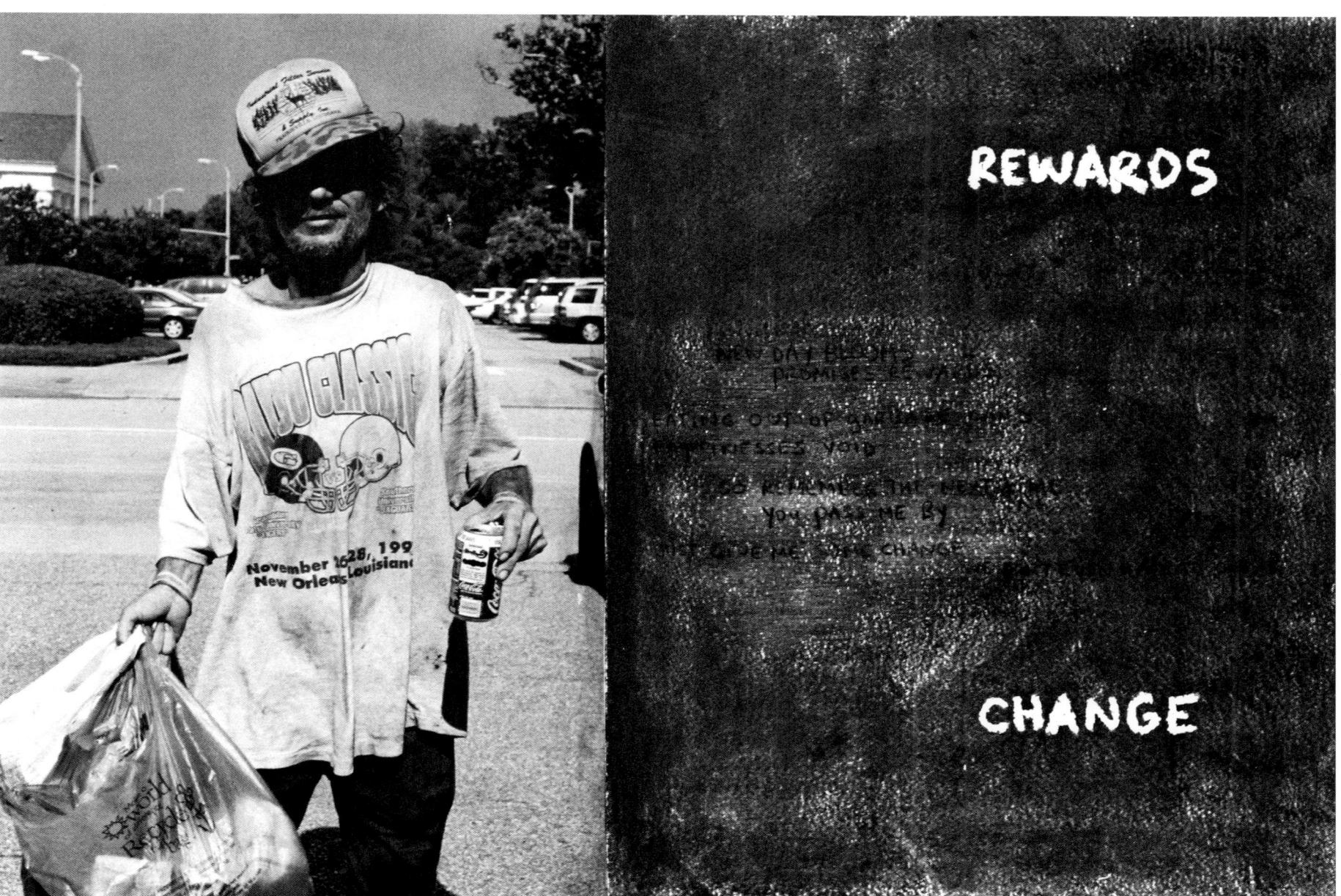

REWARDS

CHANGE

That's not what Sanders was making, though. He was making art.

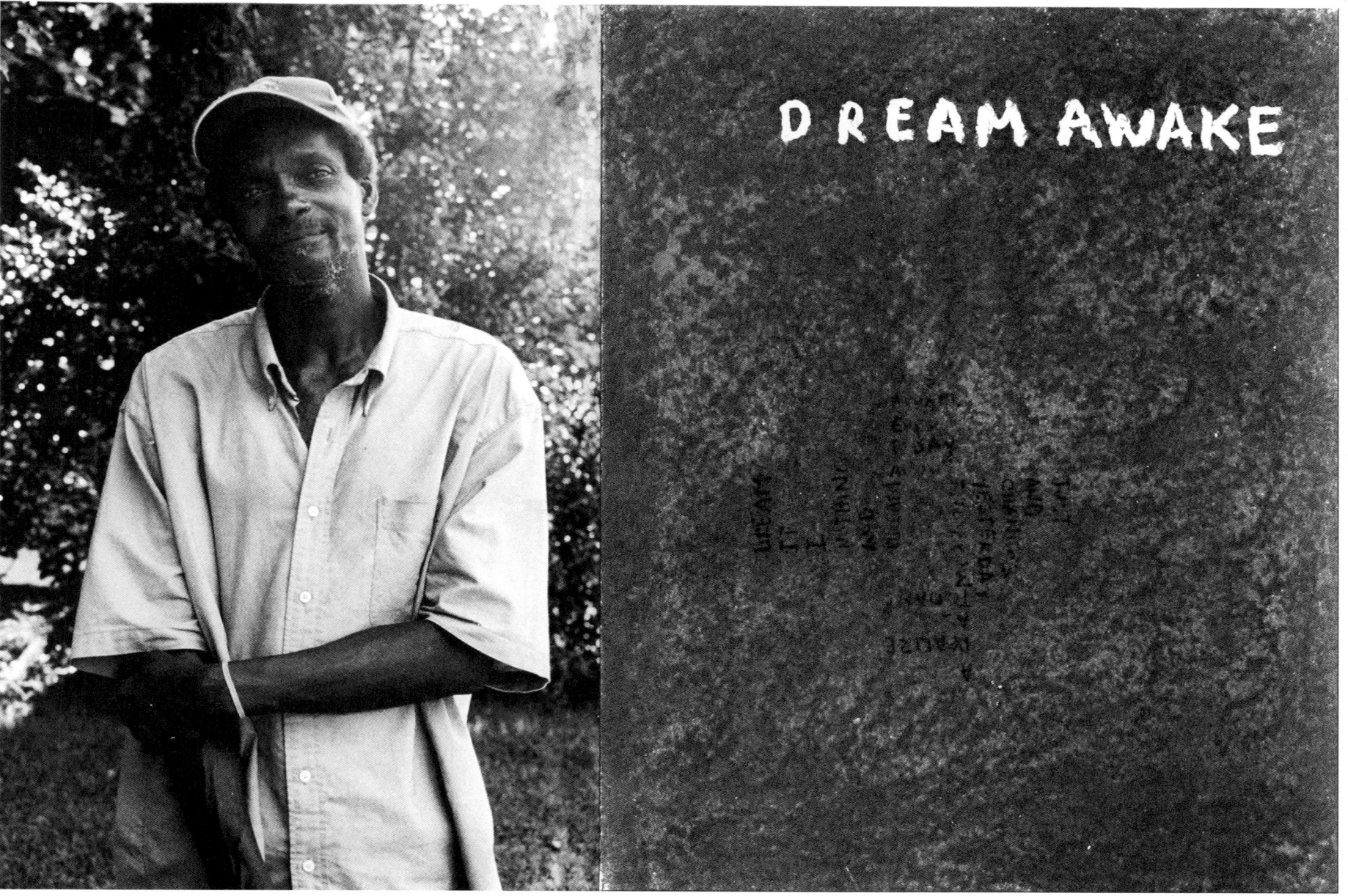

DREAM AWAKE

He was sitting crouched in front of a massive canvas in the Magazi

gallery that bears his name and where he lives

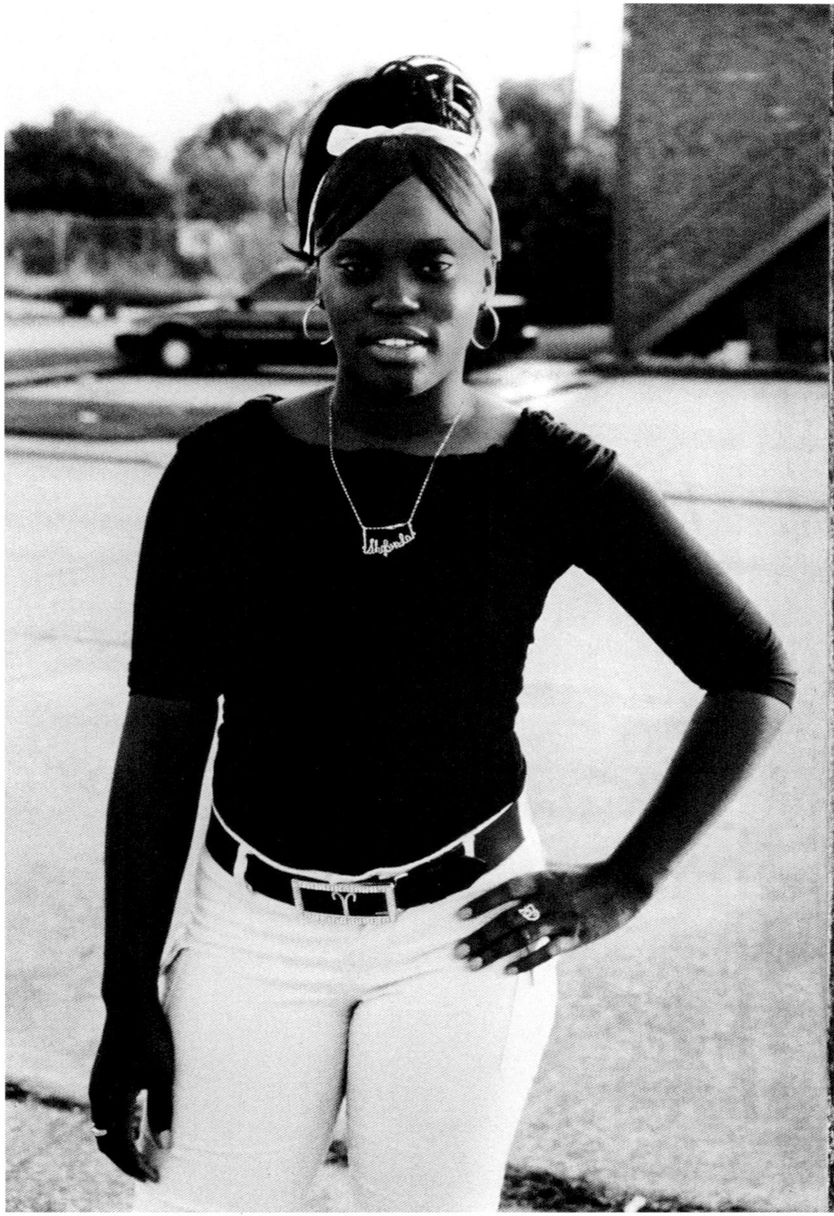

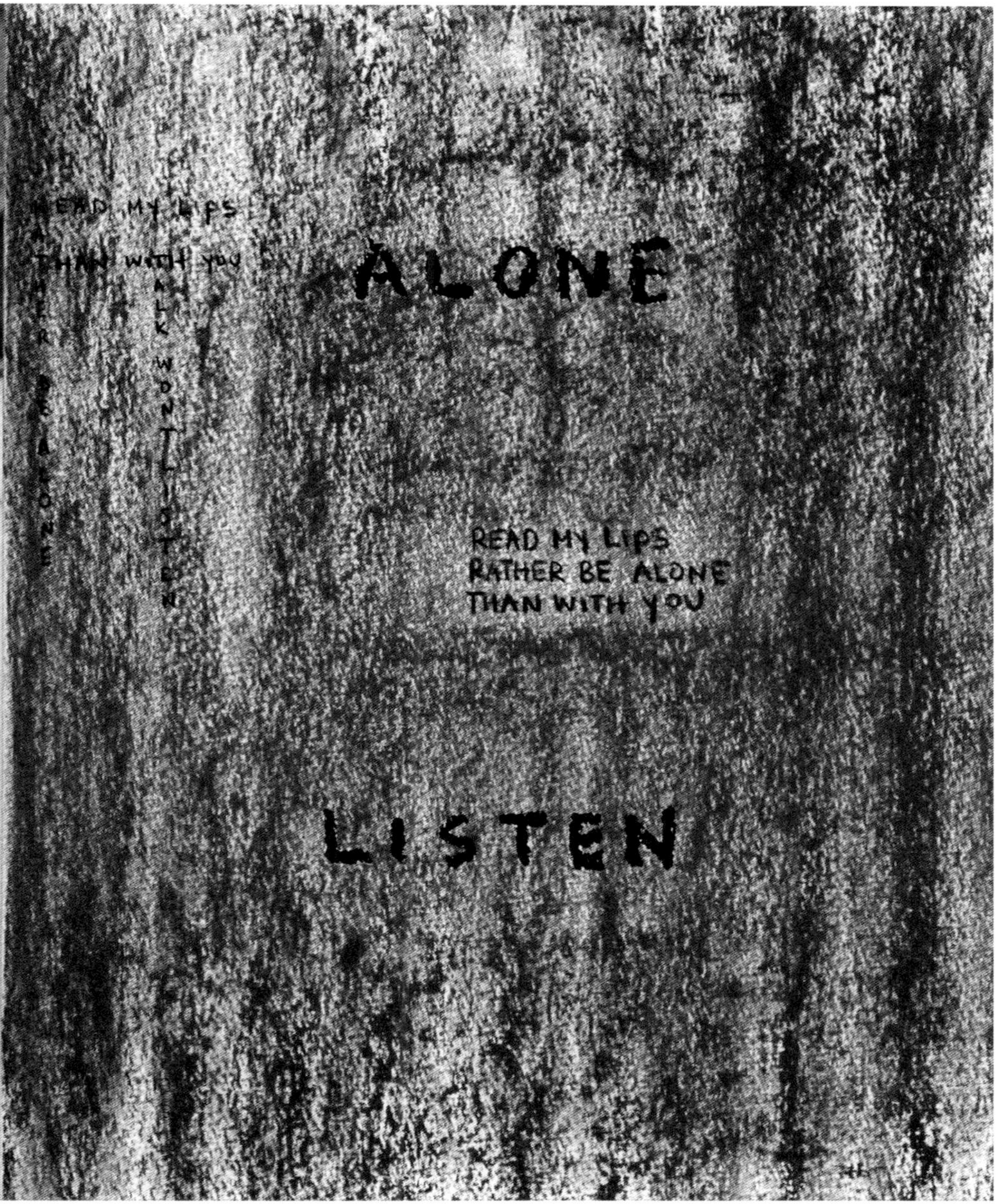
READ MY LIPS
THAN WITH YOU
ALONE
READ MY LIPS
RATHER BE ALONE
THAN WITH YOU
LISTEN

and he was putting the finishing touches on a bold, colorful painting and listening to the radio.

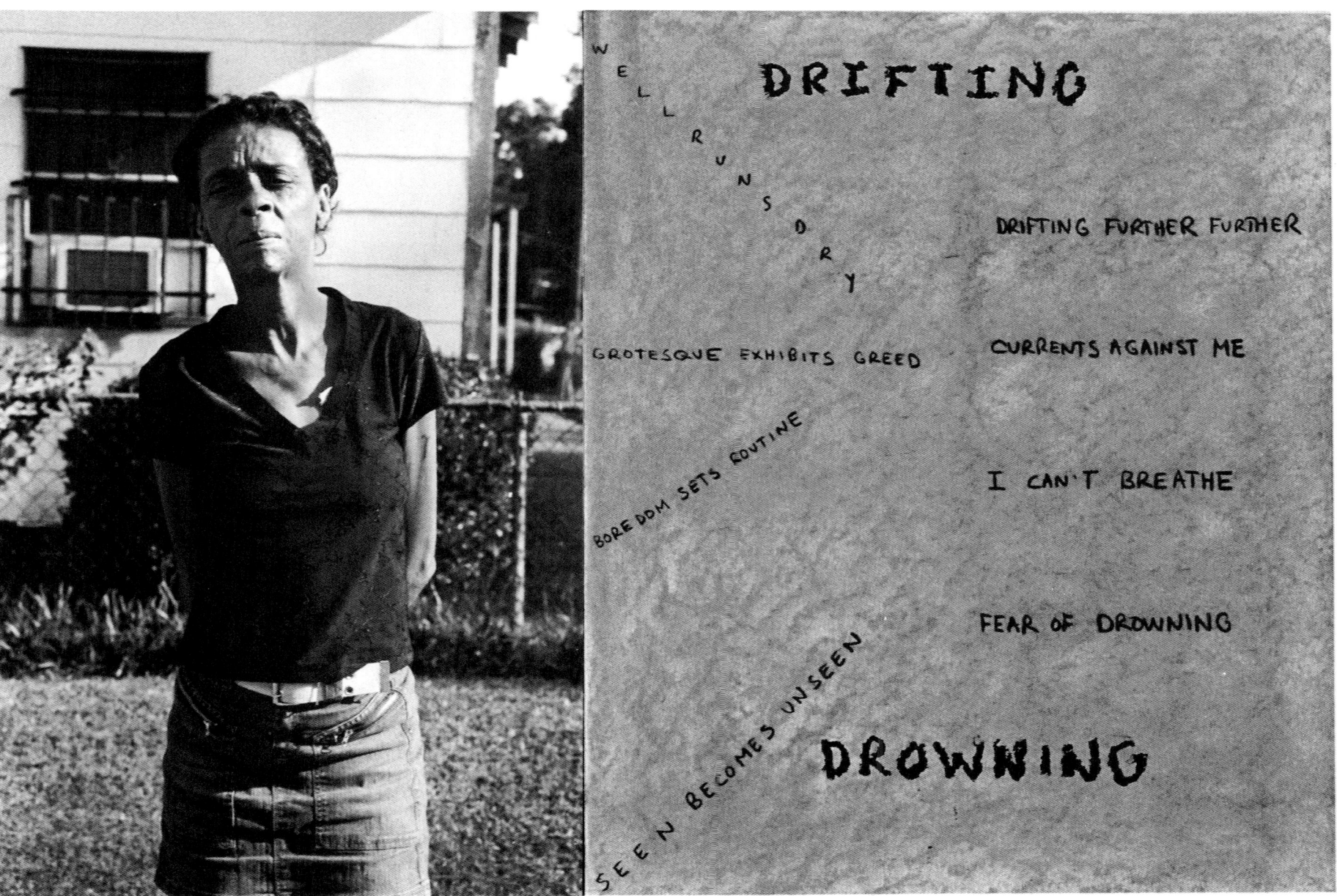

DRIFTING

WELL RUNS DRY

DRIFTING FURTHER FURTHER

GROTESQUE EXHIBITS GREED

CURRENTS AGAINST ME

BOREDOM SETS ROUTINE

I CAN'T BREATHE

FEAR OF DROWNING

SEEN BECOMES UNSEEN

DROWNING

At this point, my mental

images of New Orleanians not so mental really;

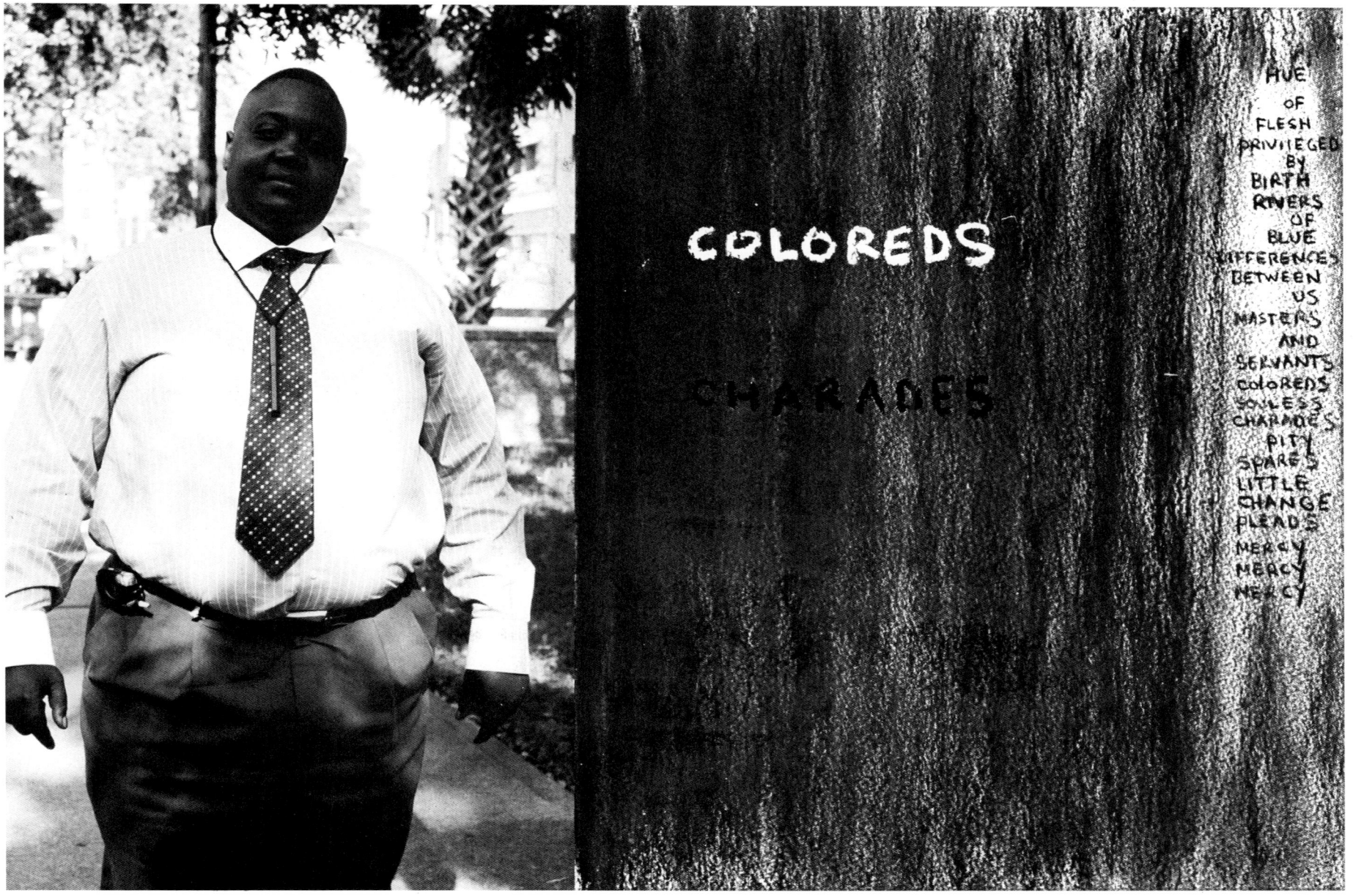

they were from TV were people dangling from choppers and dying of thirst in front of the Convention Center, and here's

this dude, painting.

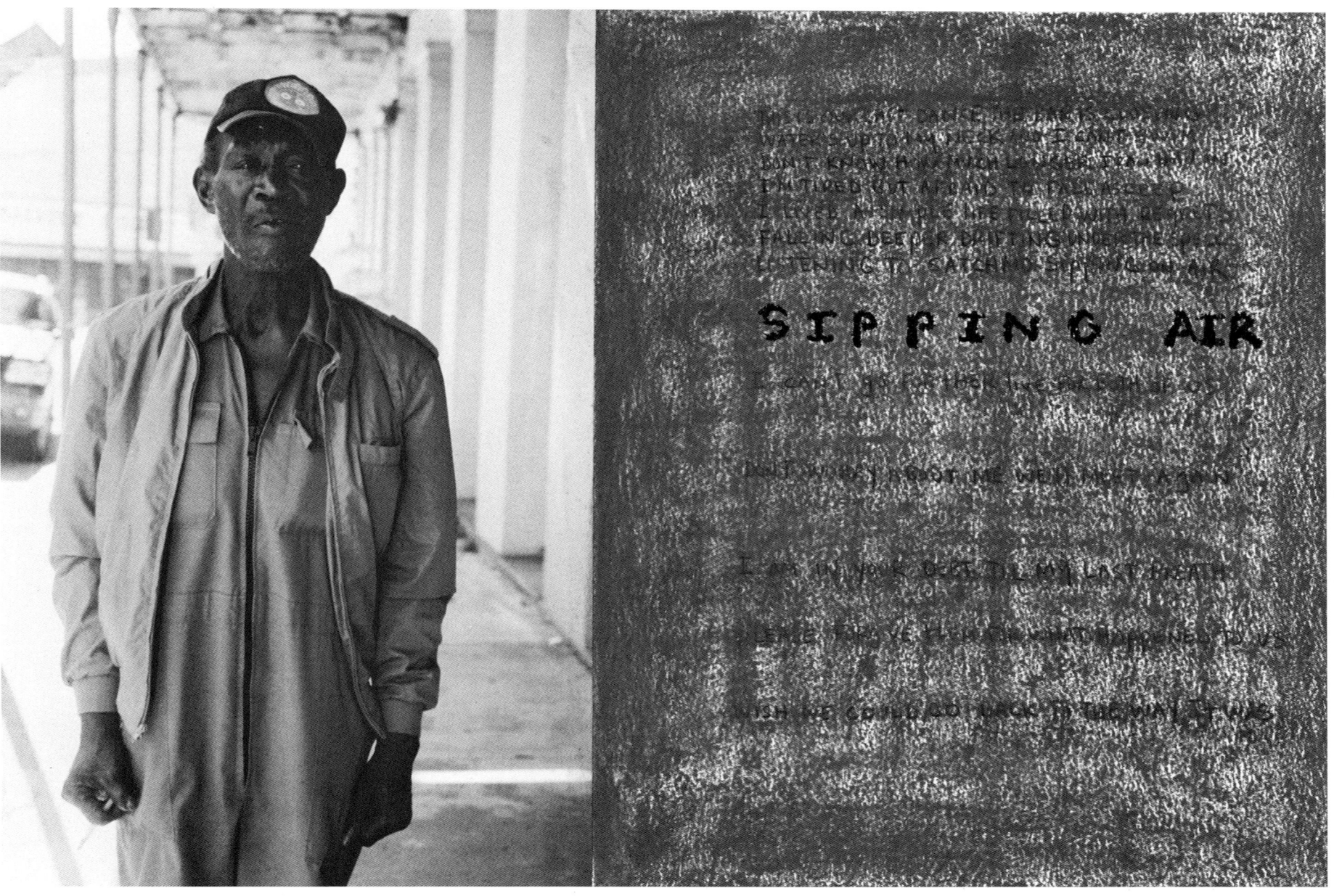

SIPPING AIR

I was thinking more about foraging for fuel and food, maybe fending off the roving gangs I had heard about -- and here's a guy making art.

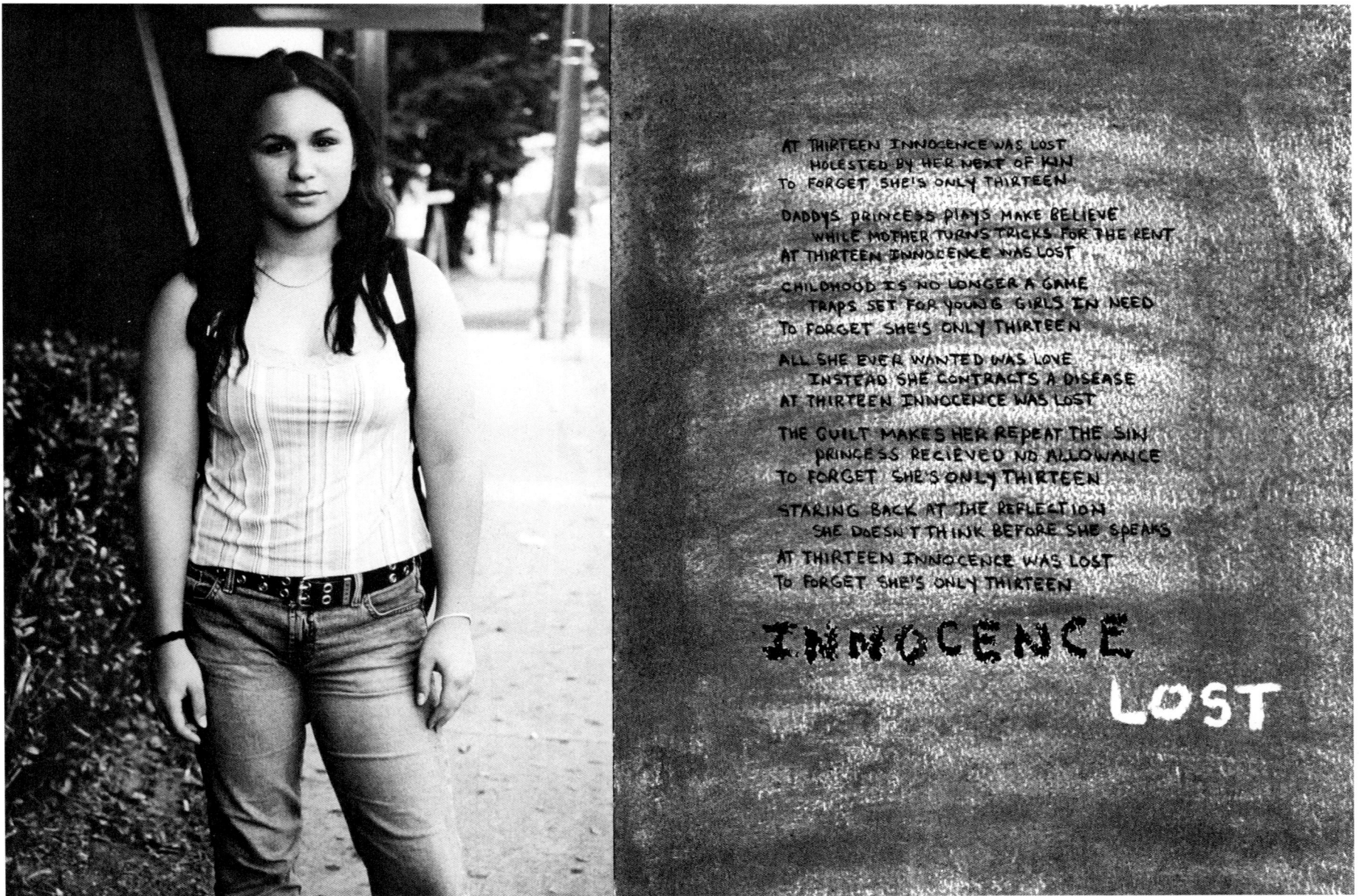

AT THIRTEEN INNOCENCE WAS LOST
    MOLESTED BY HER NEXT OF KIN
TO FORGET SHE'S ONLY THIRTEEN

DADDYS PRINCESS PLAYS MAKE BELIEVE
    WHILE MOTHER TURNS TRICKS FOR THE RENT
AT THIRTEEN INNOCENCE WAS LOST

CHILDHOOD IS NO LONGER A GAME
    TRAPS SET FOR YOUNG GIRLS IN NEED
TO FORGET SHE'S ONLY THIRTEEN

ALL SHE EVER WANTED WAS LOVE
    INSTEAD SHE CONTRACTS A DISEASE
AT THIRTEEN INNOCENCE WAS LOST

THE GUILT MAKES HER REPEAT THE SIN
    PRINCESS RECIEVED NO ALLOWANCE
TO FORGET SHE'S ONLY THIRTEEN

STARING BACK AT THE REFLECTION
    SHE DOESN'T THINK BEFORE SHE SPEAKS
AT THIRTEEN INNOCENCE WAS LOST
TO FORGET SHE'S ONLY THIRTEEN

INNOCENCE

LOST

I need to talk to this cat, I thought. So we talked.

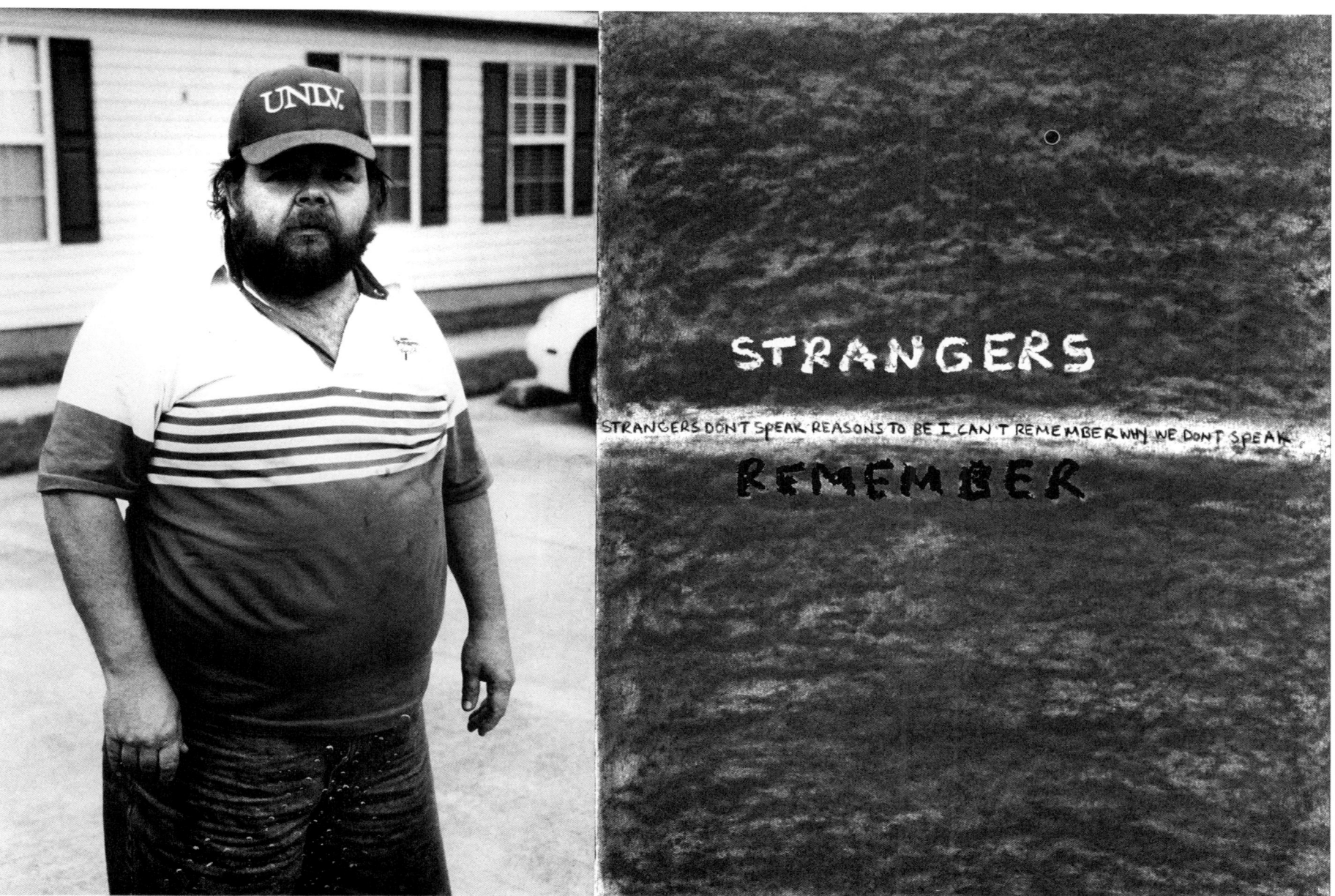

We talked about the city and we talked about art and this guy was so rock-steady -- or maybe he was flat-out nuts --

that he settled me.

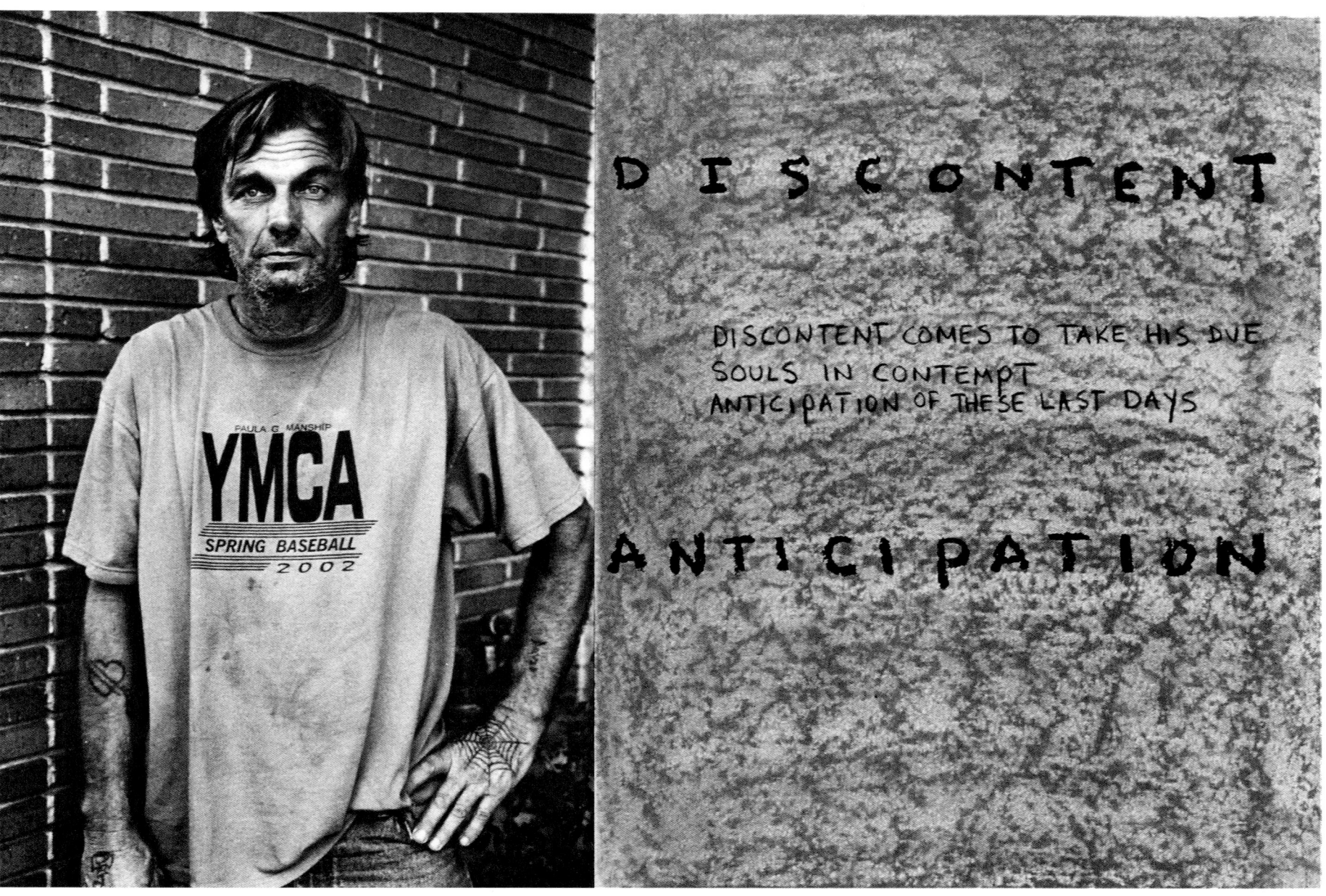

DISCONTENT

DISCONTENT COMES TO TAKE HIS DUE
SOULS IN CONTEMPT
ANTICIPATION OF THESE LAST DAYS

ANTICIPATION

Like many of the more eccentric characters in this city, he's not from New Orleans (born in Pineville, actually) but settled here about a year ago after a young life traveling the globe because it feels like home.

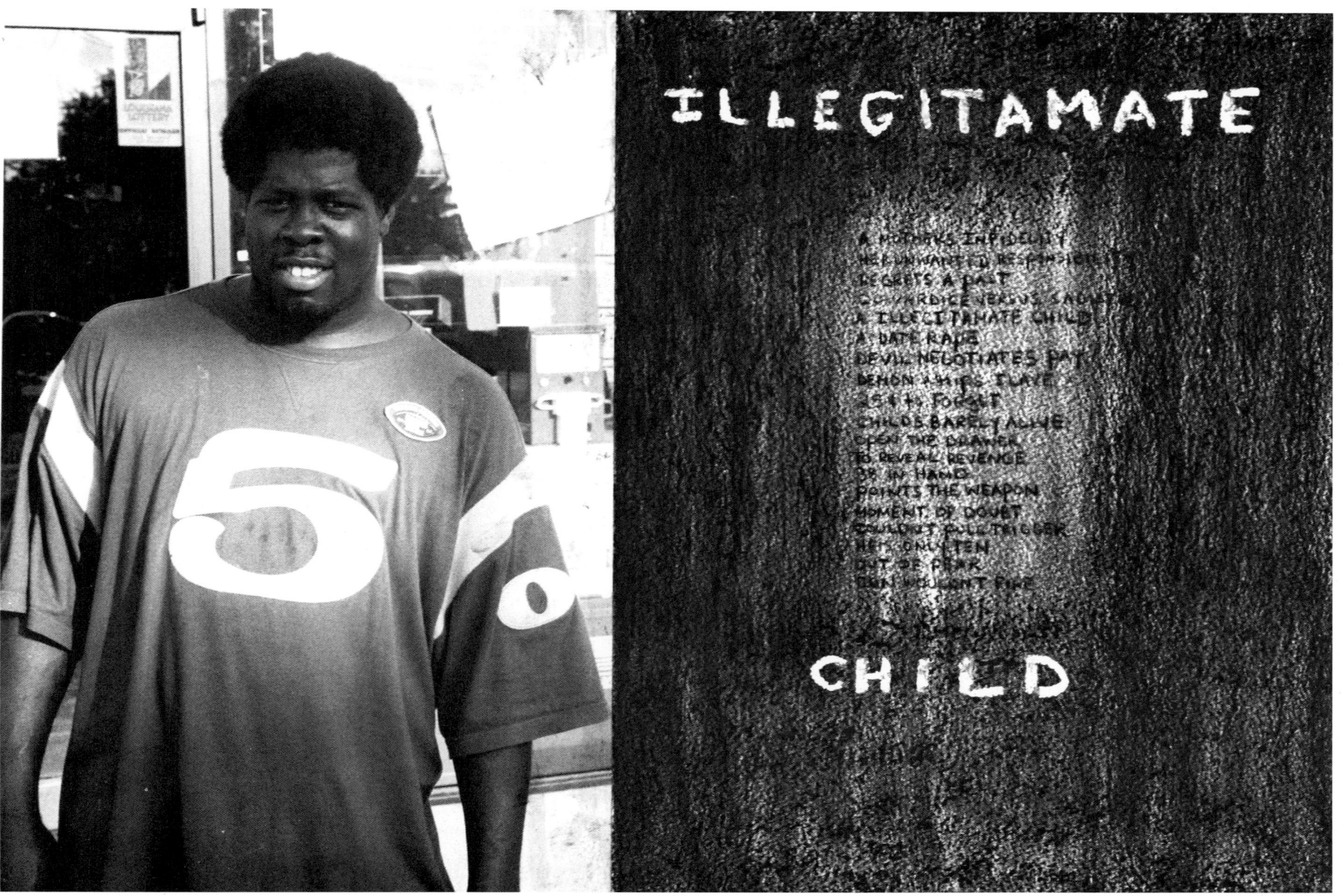

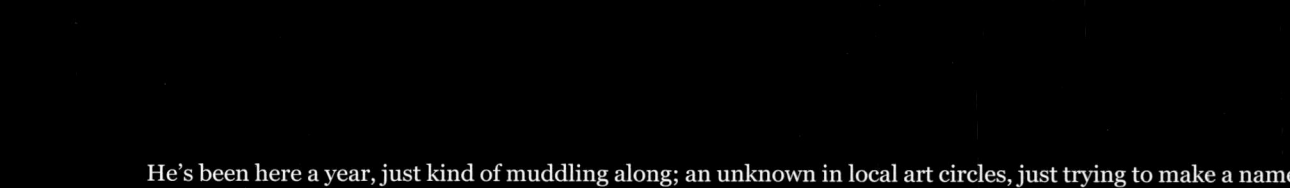

He's been here a year, just kind of muddling along; an unknown in local art circles, just trying to make a name.

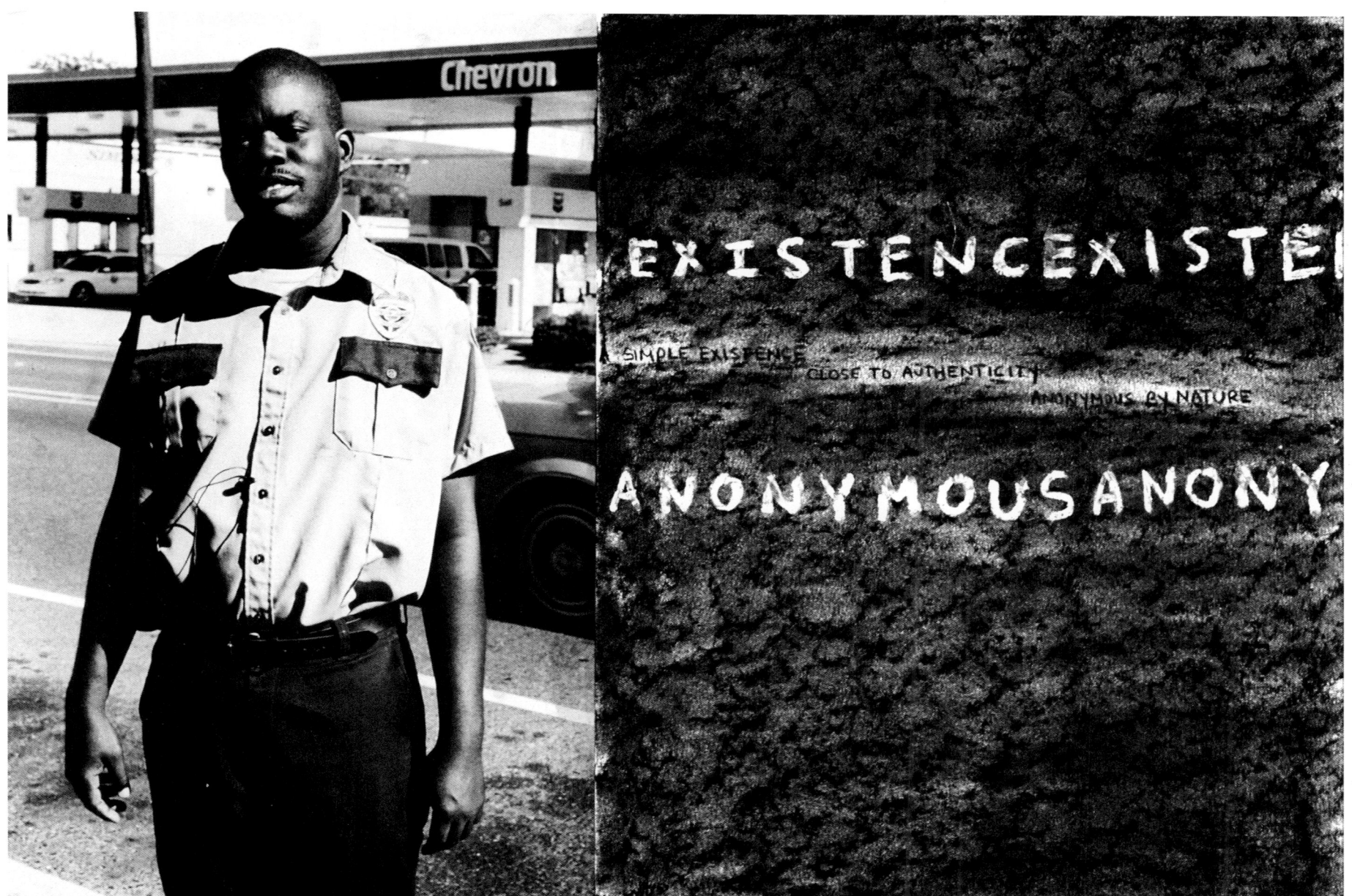

And here's the thing about the painting he was working on:

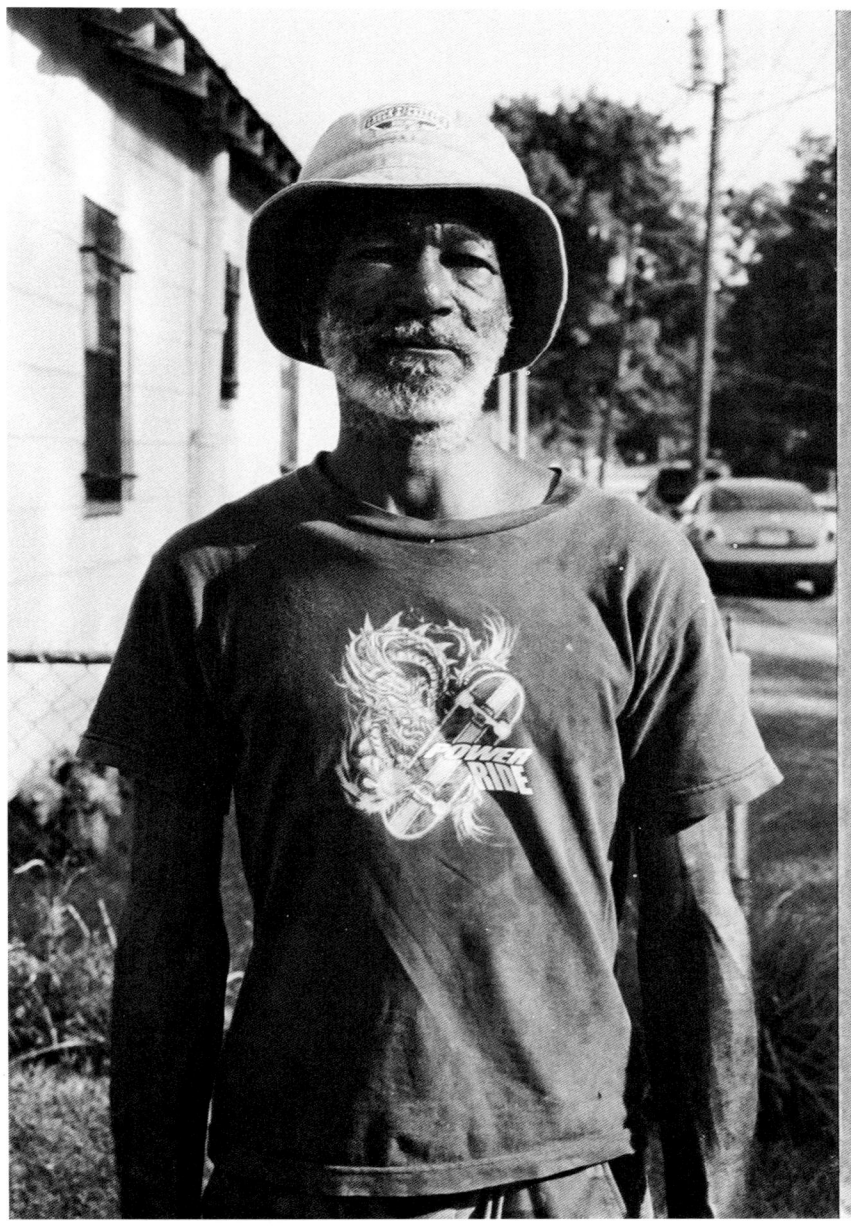

AS QUESTIONS GO UNANSWERED

AS HOPE IS ABANDONED

AS HUMAN KINDNESS IS REVERED

AS THE DEPTHS OF THE SENSES
ARE FURTHER JADED

AS RIVERS FLOW FROM THE WINDOWS
OF THE SOUL

QUESTIONS

AS I REMAIN QUIET WITH HUMILITY
AND DISREGARD

UNANSWERED

It was the final panel of a series he had been working on for four years, a commemoration -- of all things -- of the Sept. 11 disaster.

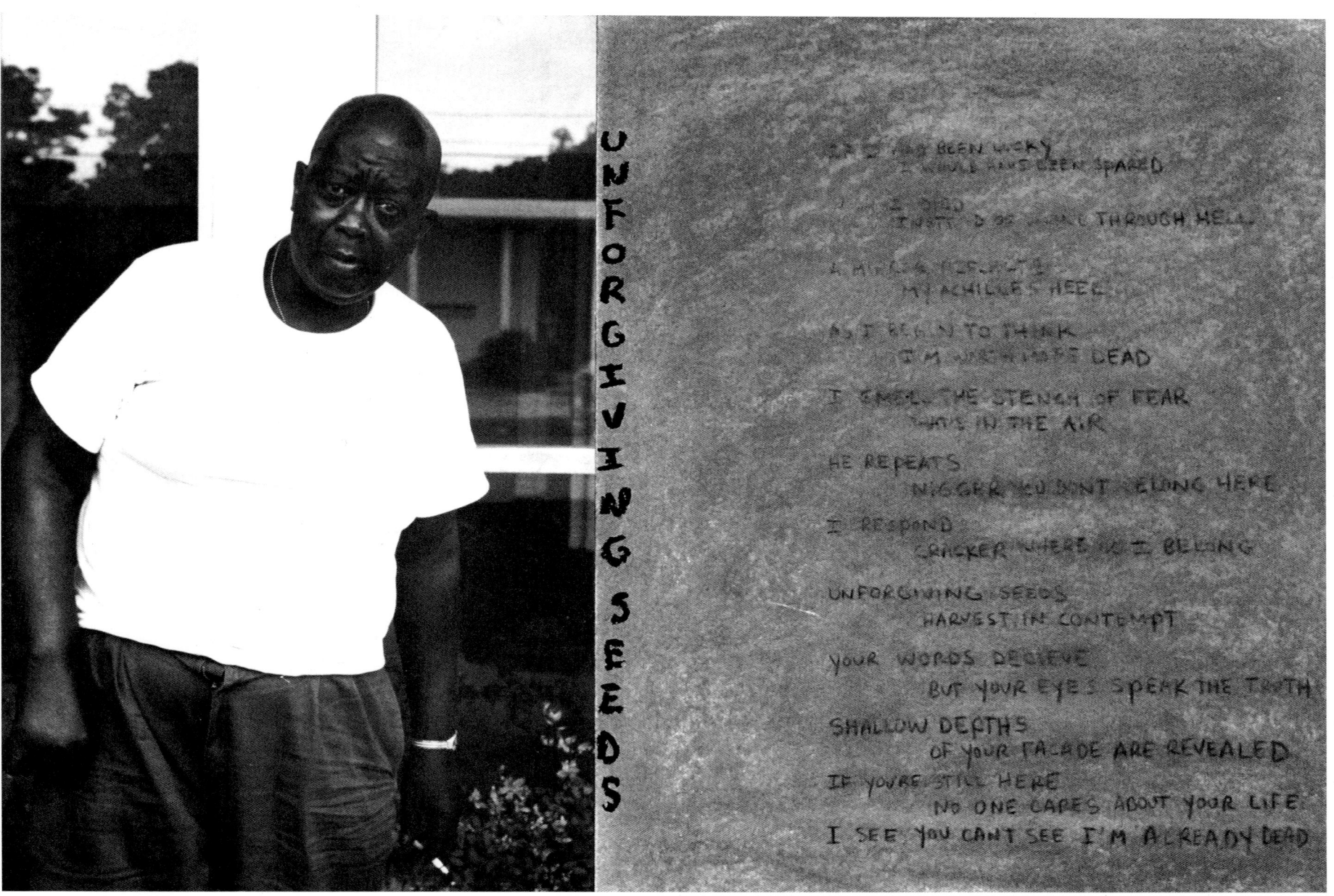

UNFORGIVING SEEDS

HAD YOU BEEN LUCKY
    I WOULD HAVE BEEN SPARED

IF I DIED
    THAT'S TO BE DONE THROUGH HELL

A MAN'S WEAKNESS
    MY ACHILLES HEEL

AS I BEGIN TO THINK
    I'M WORTH MORE DEAD

I SMELL THE STENCH OF FEAR
    THAT'S IN THE AIR

HE REPEATS
    NIGGER YOU DON'T BELONG HERE

I RESPOND
    CRACKER WHERE DO I BELONG

UNFORGIVING SEEDS
    HARVEST IN CONTEMPT

YOUR WORDS DECIEVE
    BUT YOUR EYES SPEAK THE TRUTH

SHALLOW DEPTHS
    OF YOUR FACADE ARE REVEALED

IF YOU'RE STILL HERE
    NO ONE CARES ABOUT YOUR LIFE

I SEE YOU CAN'T SEE I'M ALREADY DEAD

It was a list of the names of the dead.

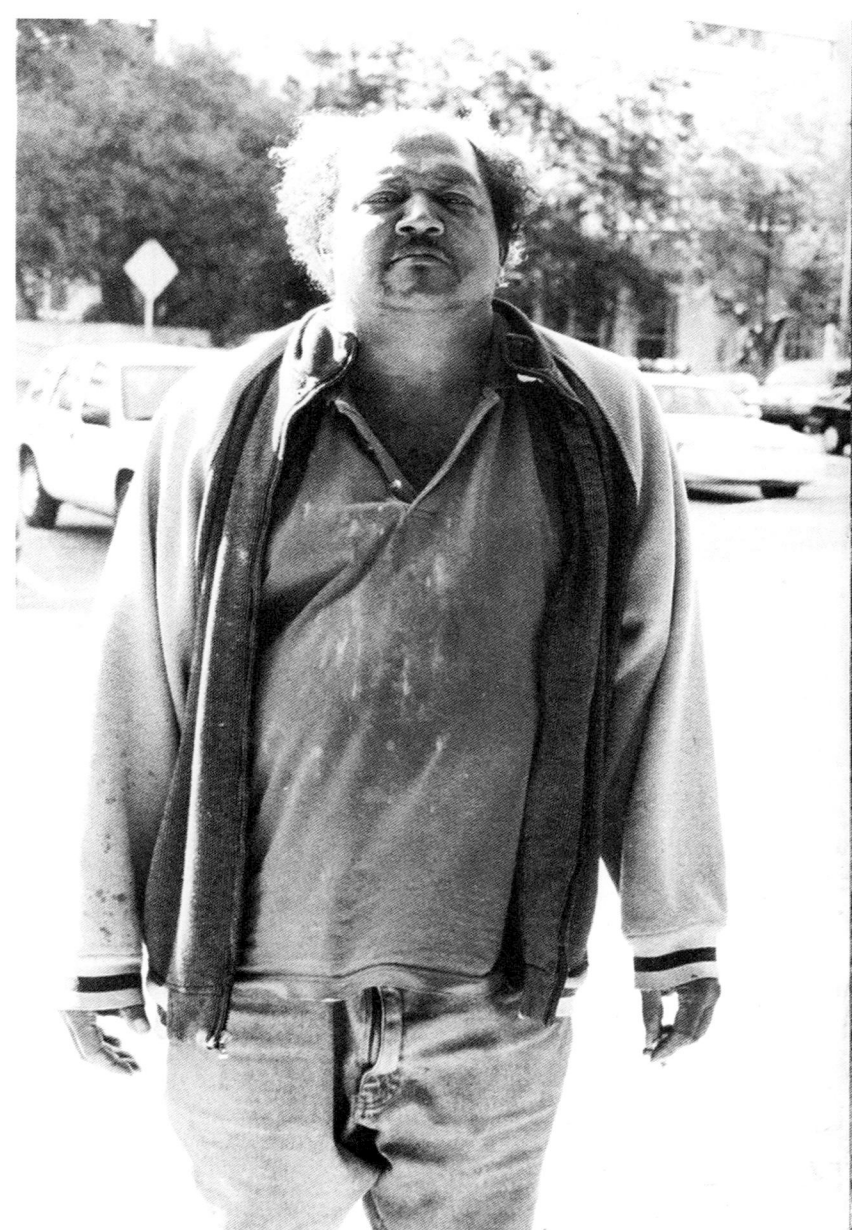

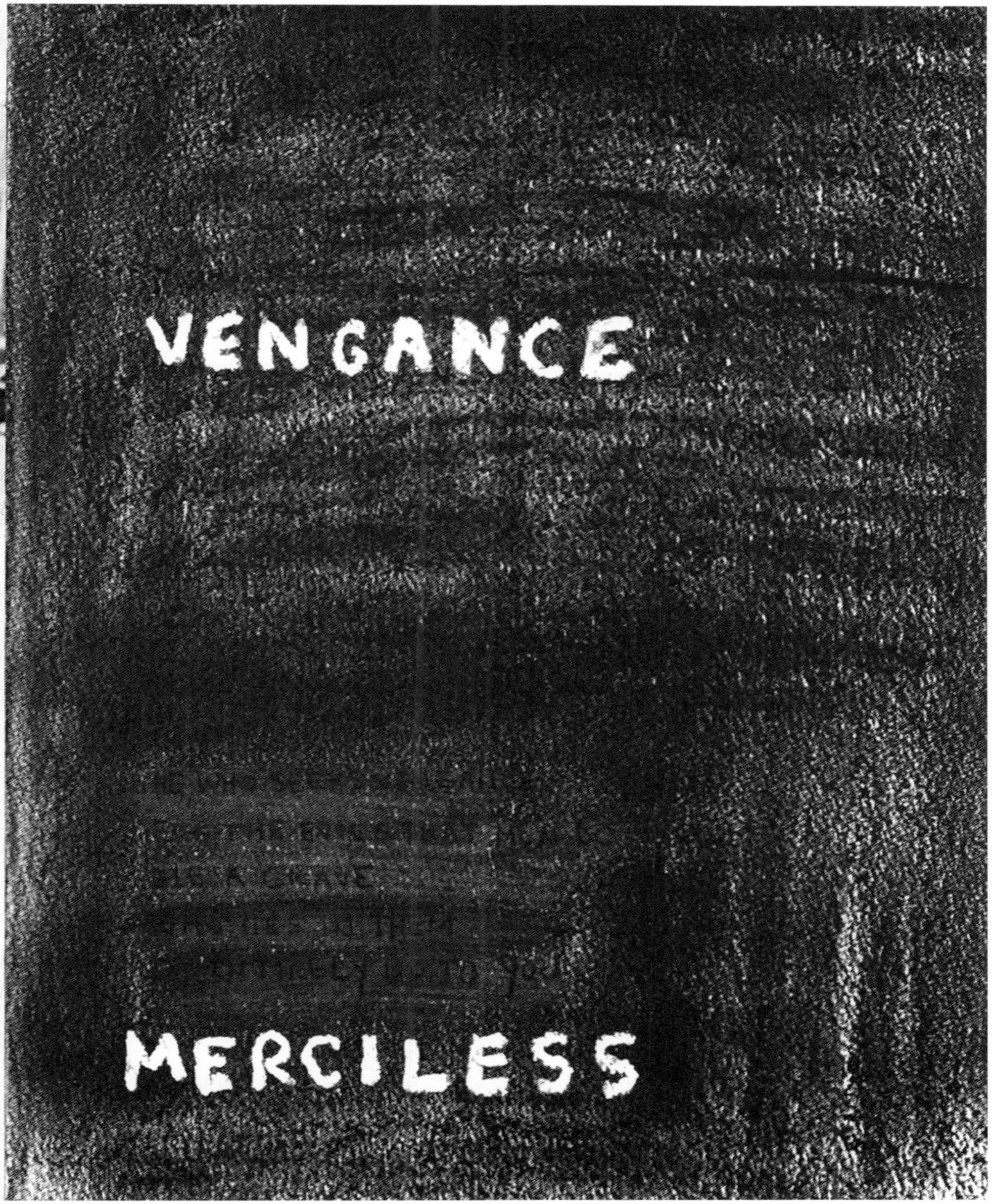

VENGANCE

MERCILESS

Well, if you're a fan of irony. . . . I glibly remarked that he shouldn't have any trouble finding subject matter for his next project.

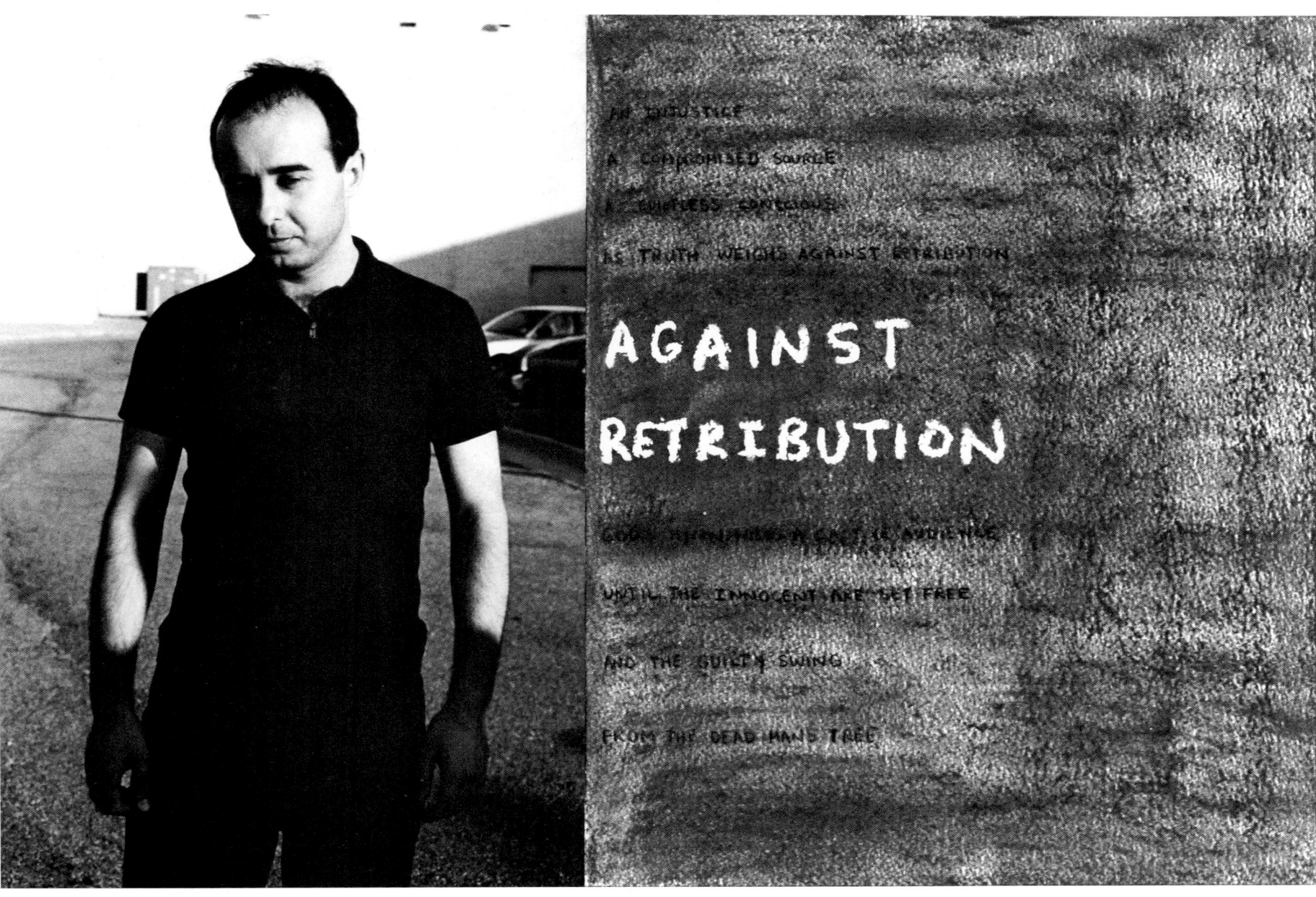

"Yeah," he said. "Disaster can be like that. It makes death, despair . . . and art."

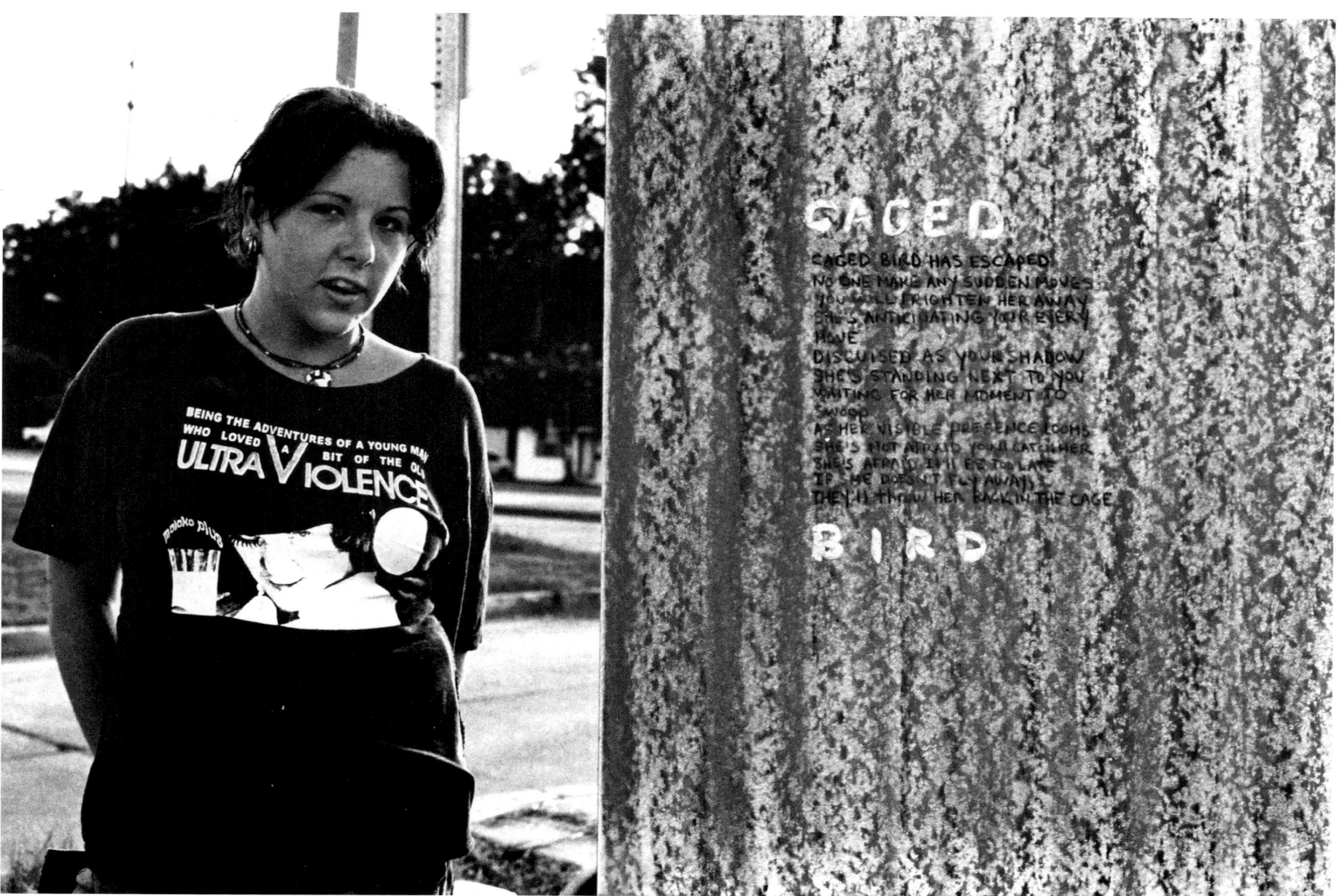

CAGED

CAGED BIRD HAS ESCAPED!
NO ONE MAKE ANY SUDDEN MOVES
YOU WILL FRIGHTEN HER AWAY
SHE'S ANTICIPATING YOUR EVERY
MOVE
DISGUISED AS YOUR SHADOW
SHE'S STANDING NEXT TO YOU
WAITING FOR HER MOMENT TO
SWOOP
AS HER VISIBLE PRESENCE LOOMS
SHE'S NOT AFRAID YOU'LL CATCH HER
SHE'S AFRAID IF I'LL BE TOO LATE
IF SHE DOESN'T FLY AWAY
THEY'LL THROW HER BACK IN THE CAGE

BIRD

He told me this week, all these months later: "I felt like an obscure guy in a lost place.

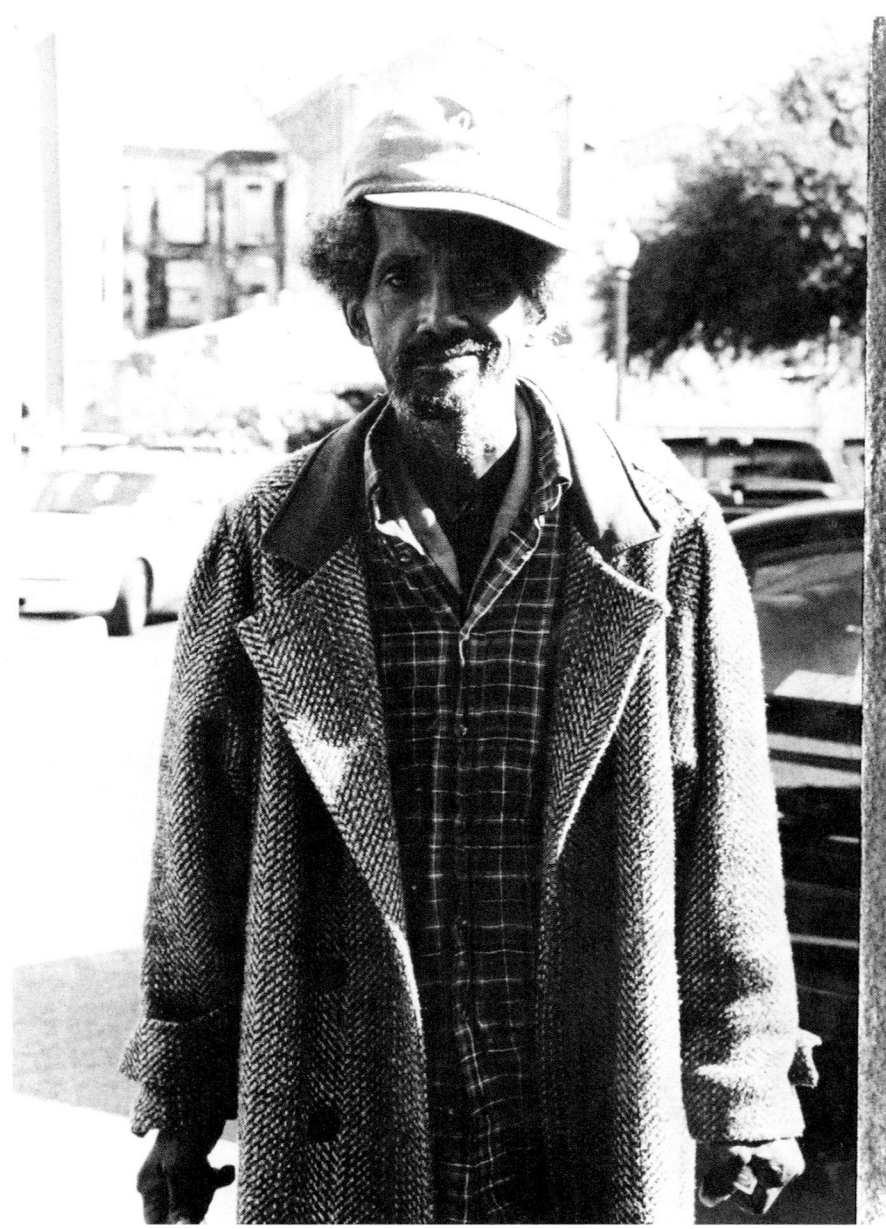

CONSEQUENCES

HE DEALS ONE FOR ME
        TWO FOR HIM
I PLAY THE CARDS
        I'M DEALT TO LOSE
YOU BUY AND SELL
        YOUR BELLY IS FULL
YOU DEVOUR EVERYTHING
        I'M WITHOUT FOOD
ENGULFED IN ANIMOSITY
        CONSEQUENCES OF SIX DEGREES
DECIPHER THE MYSTERY
        MASTERS GREATEST SCHEME
ONE DAY I WILL BE THE MASTER
        AND YOU WILL BE SERVING ME

ENGULFED

There was all this hell going on. I was just trying to find some inner peace."

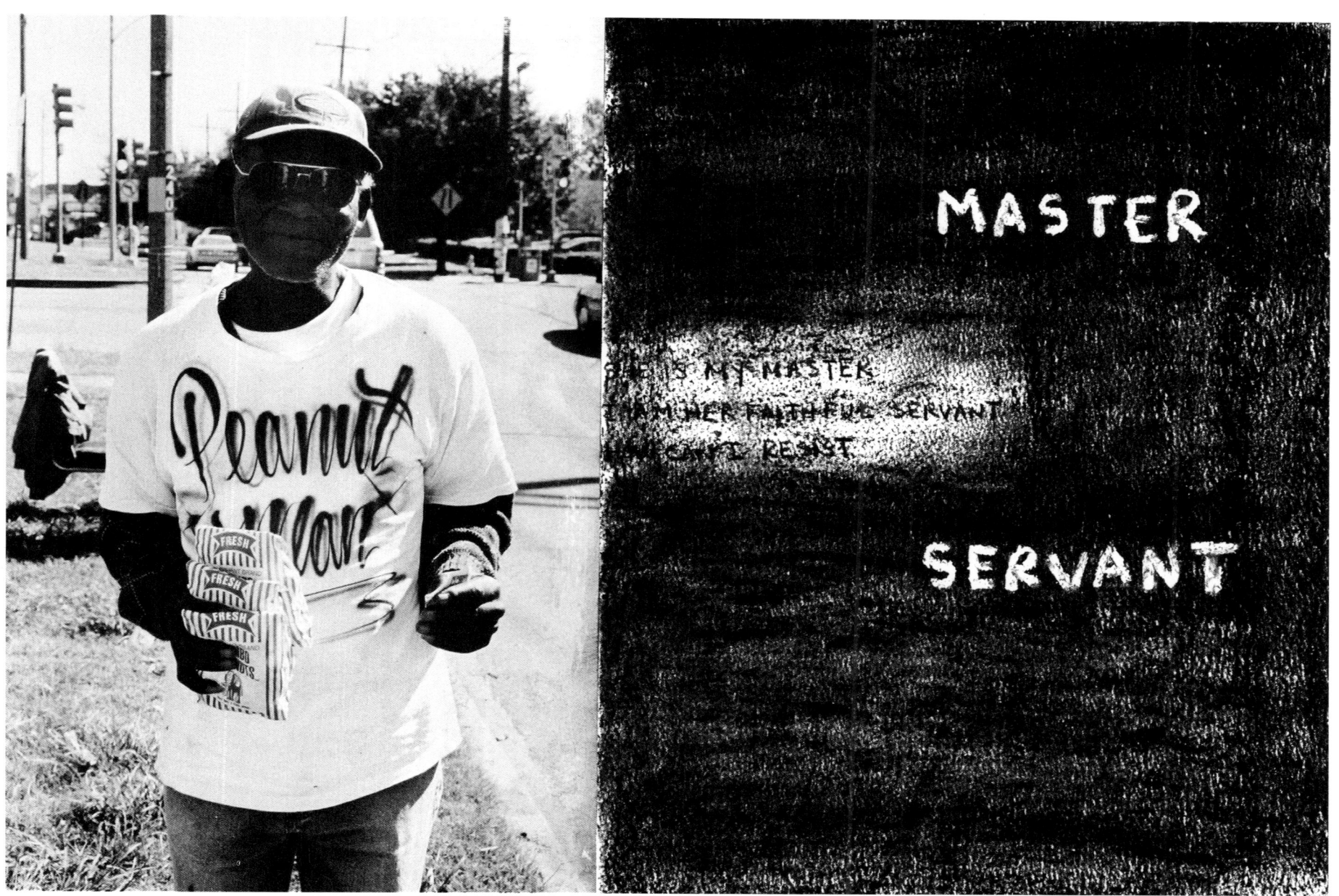

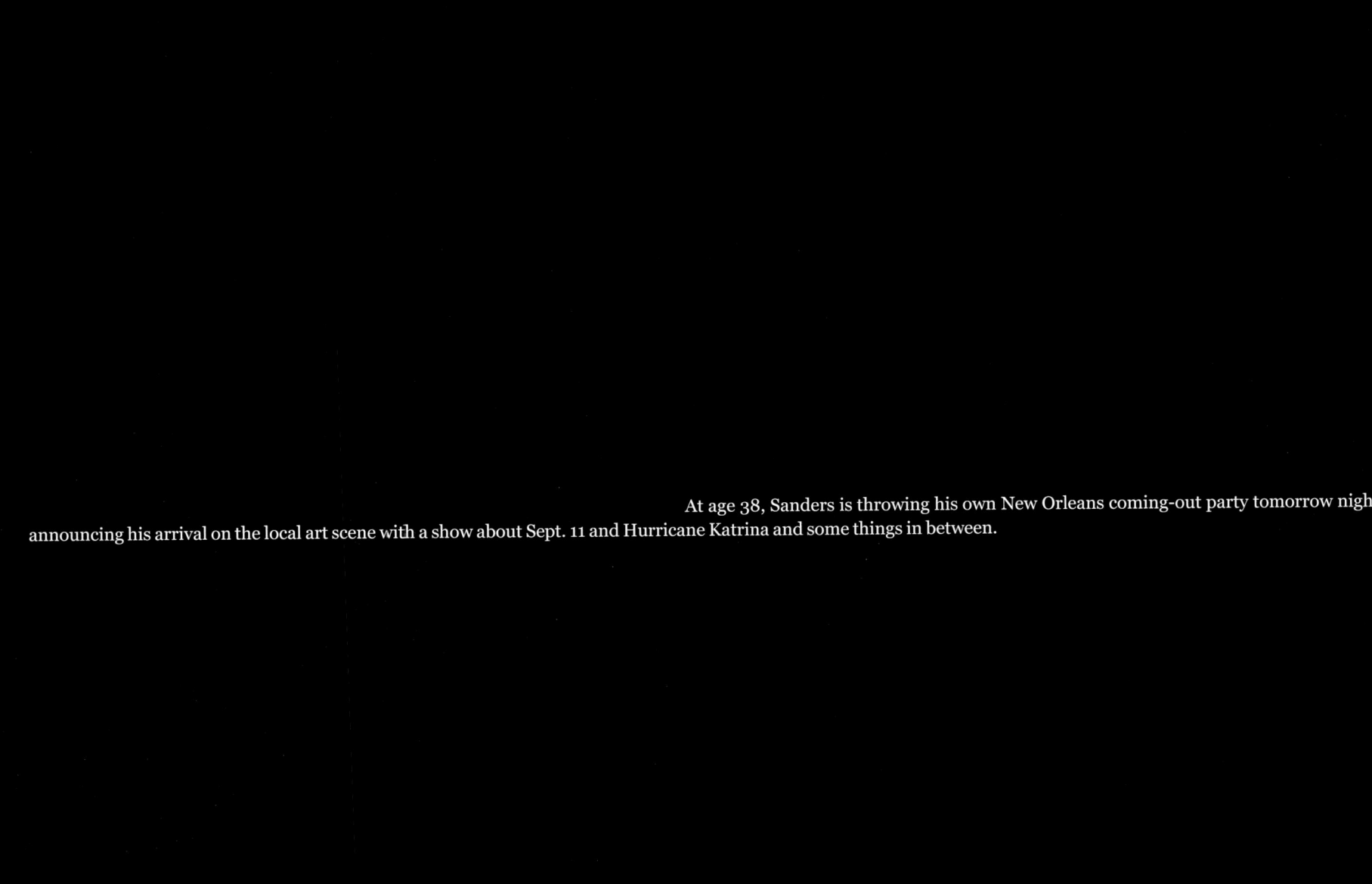

At age 38, Sanders is throwing his own New Orleans coming-out party tomorrow night announcing his arrival on the local art scene with a show about Sept. 11 and Hurricane Katrina and some things in between.

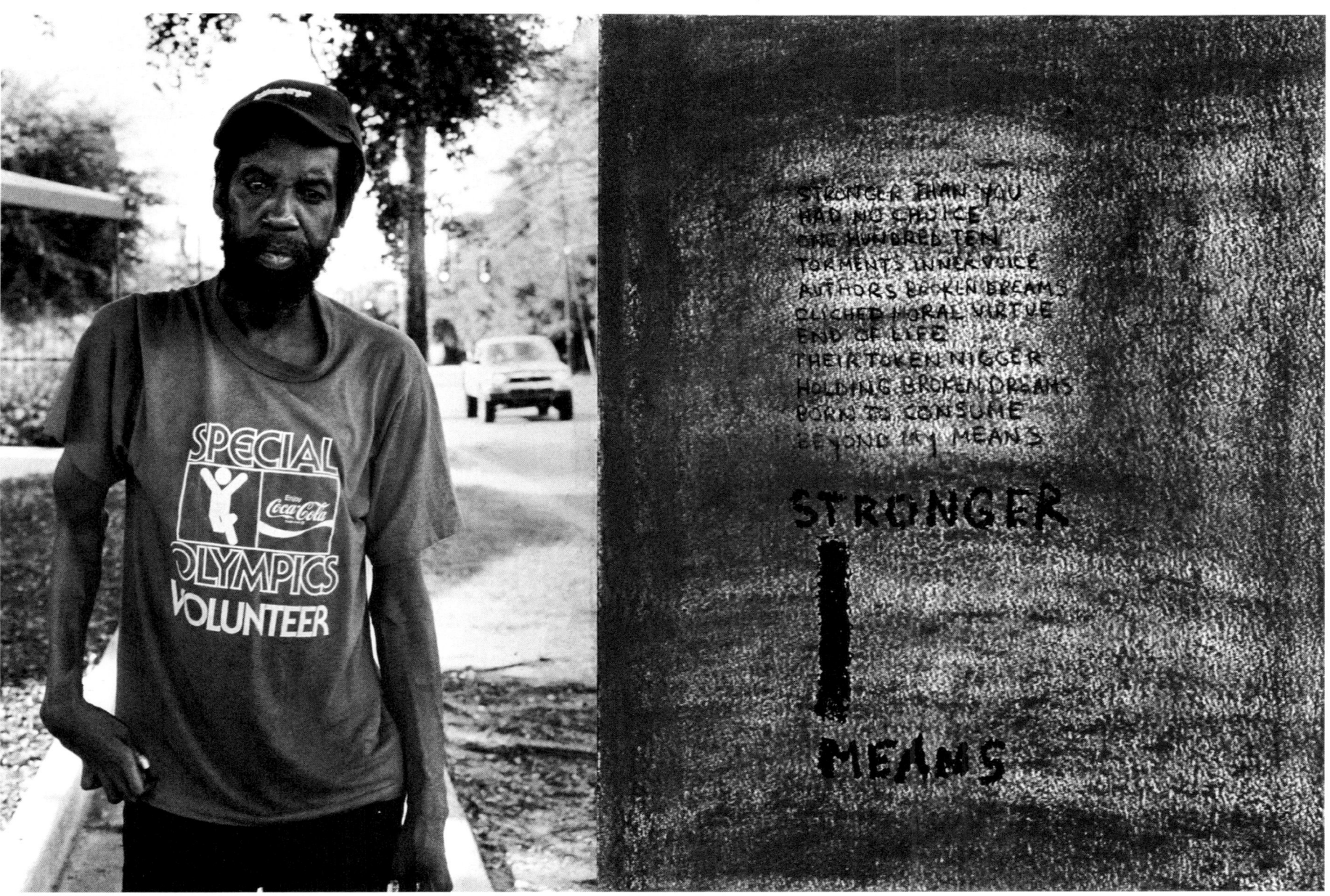

57

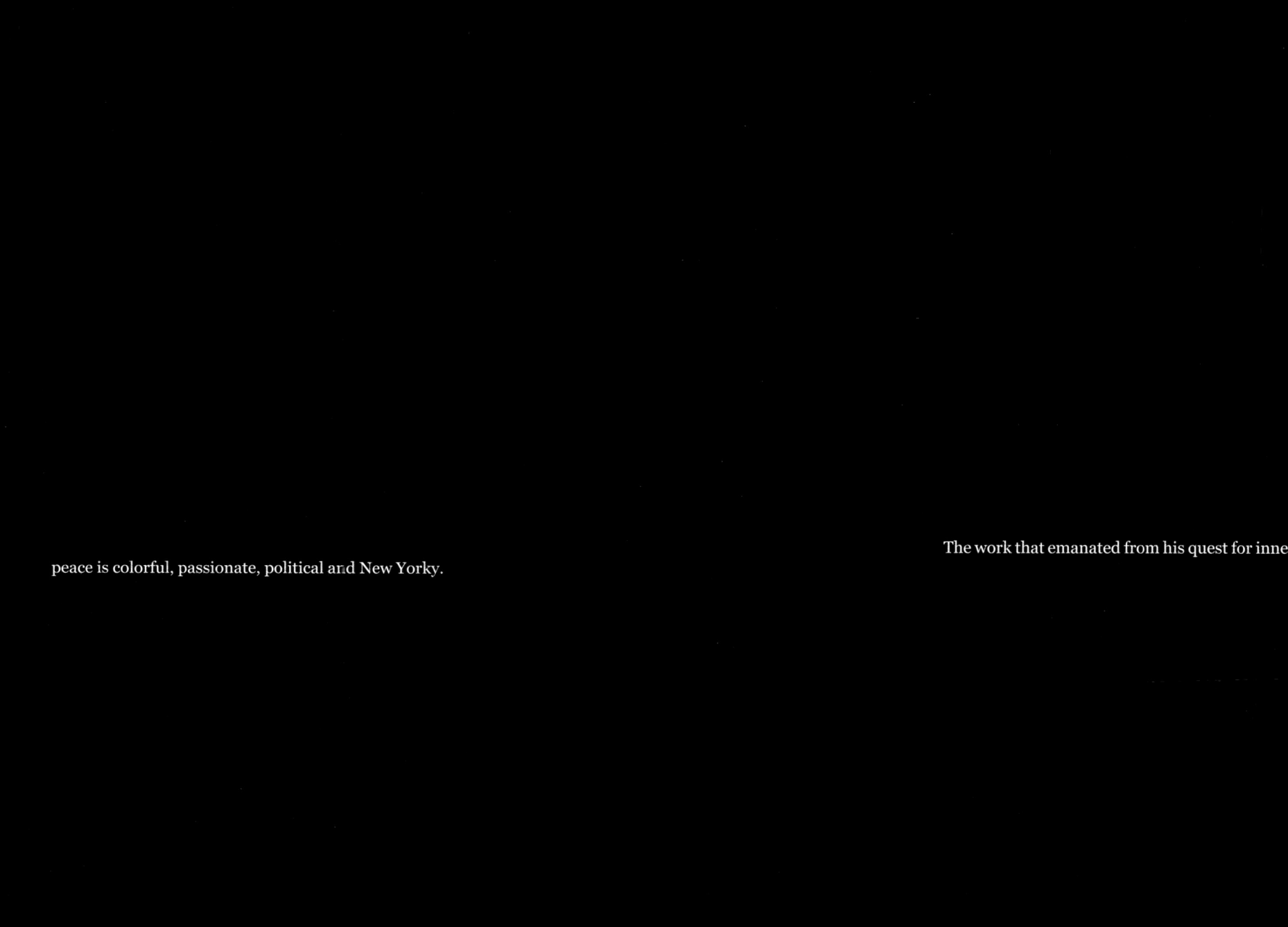

peace is colorful, passionate, political and New Yorky.

The work that emanated from his quest for inner

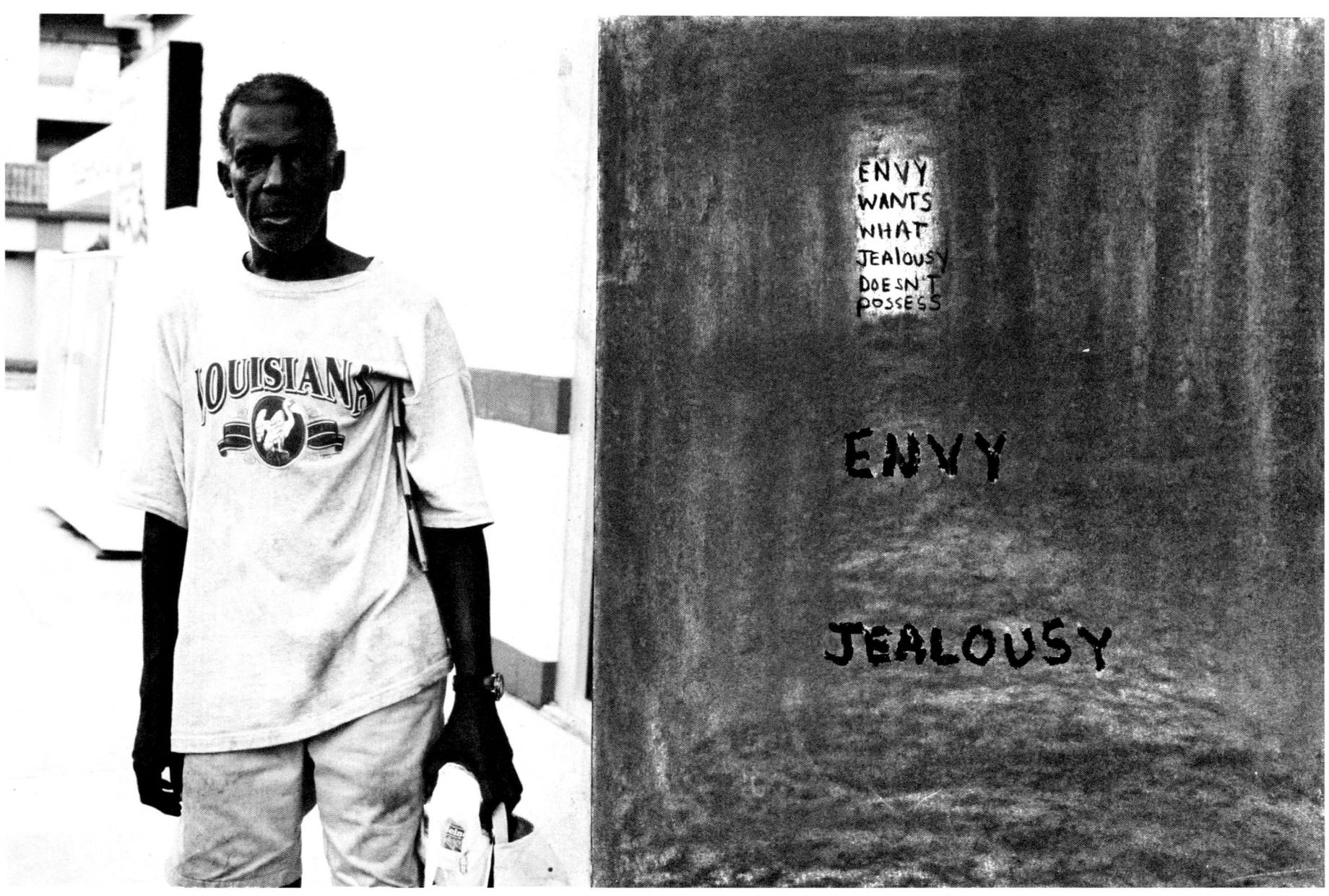

He used to run in Basquiat's crown in Gotham City; maybe that's an influence.

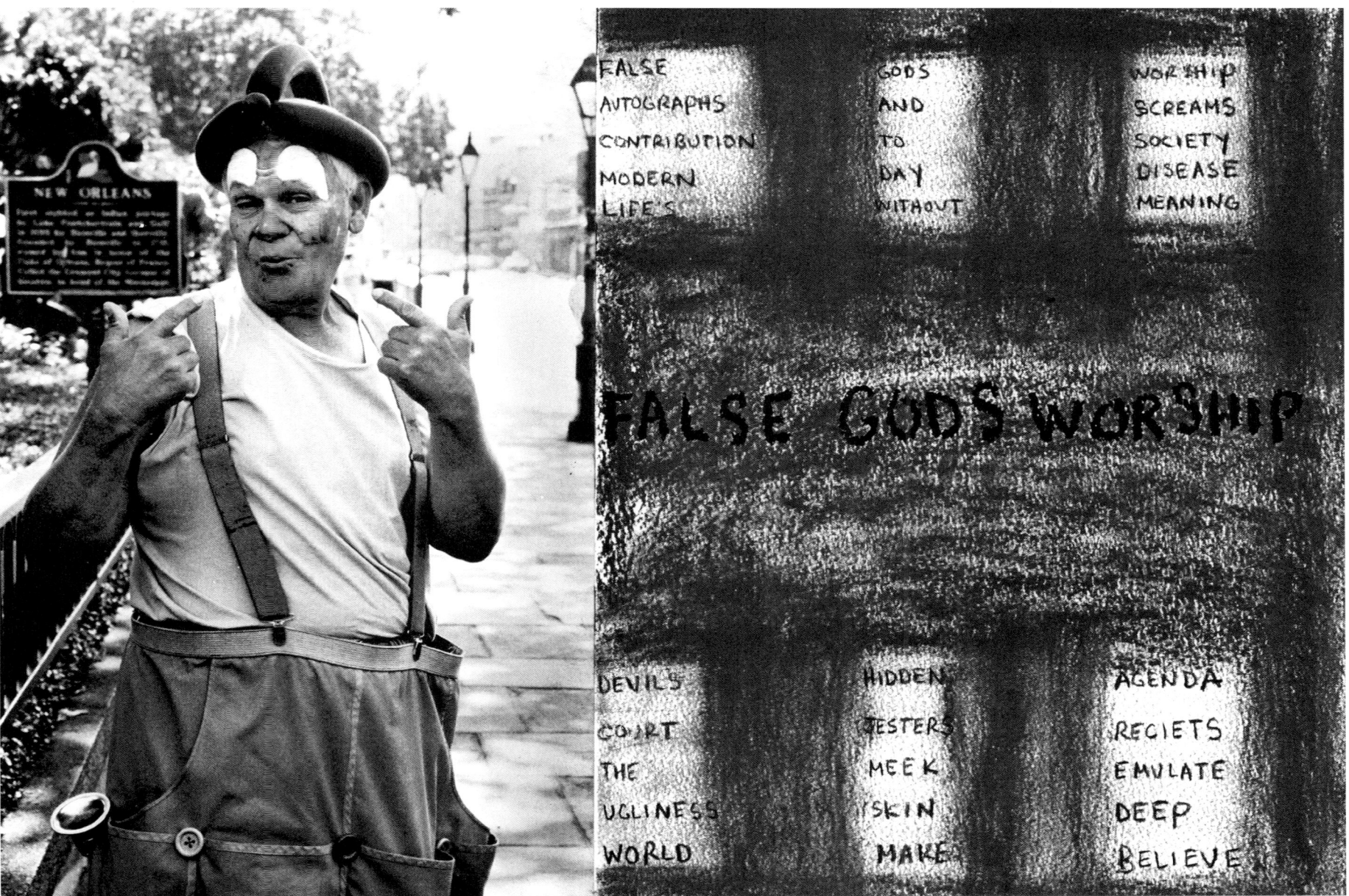

61

There's lots of text, for those who like to read their paintings.

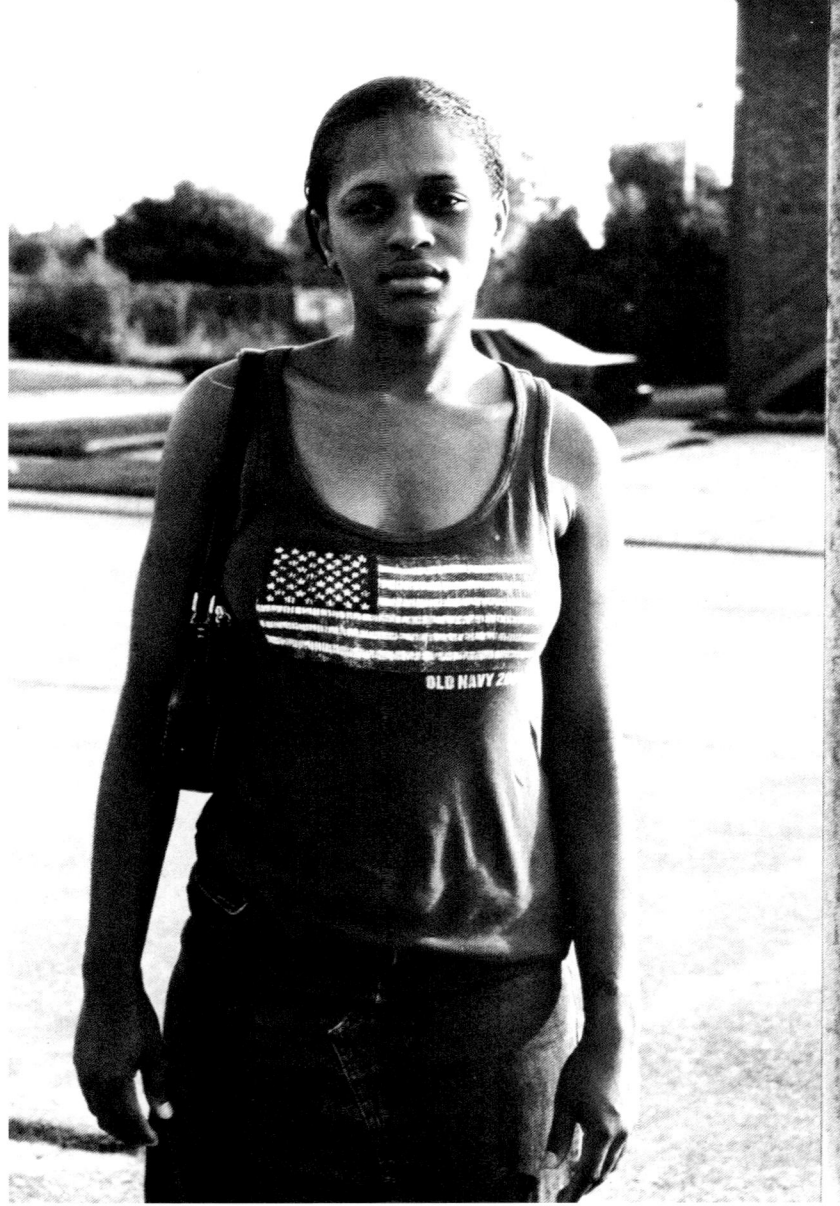

MYSTERY

MYSTERY OF YOU
STIRS MY EMOTIONS
BEAUTY OVERSHADOWS
RISKING MY LIFE
FOR ONE MOMENT
THEN ALL'S LOST
AS I REMEMBER
SCENT OF DESIRE
IN MY ARMS
RELIVING THE PAST
FORGETTING THE PRESENT
LONLINESS SEEPS INSIDE
TO BE WANTED
ALL I ASK

I'M CONSTANTLY DENIED

DENIED

There are stark photos he took of passengers when he was a cabdriver in Baton Rouge.

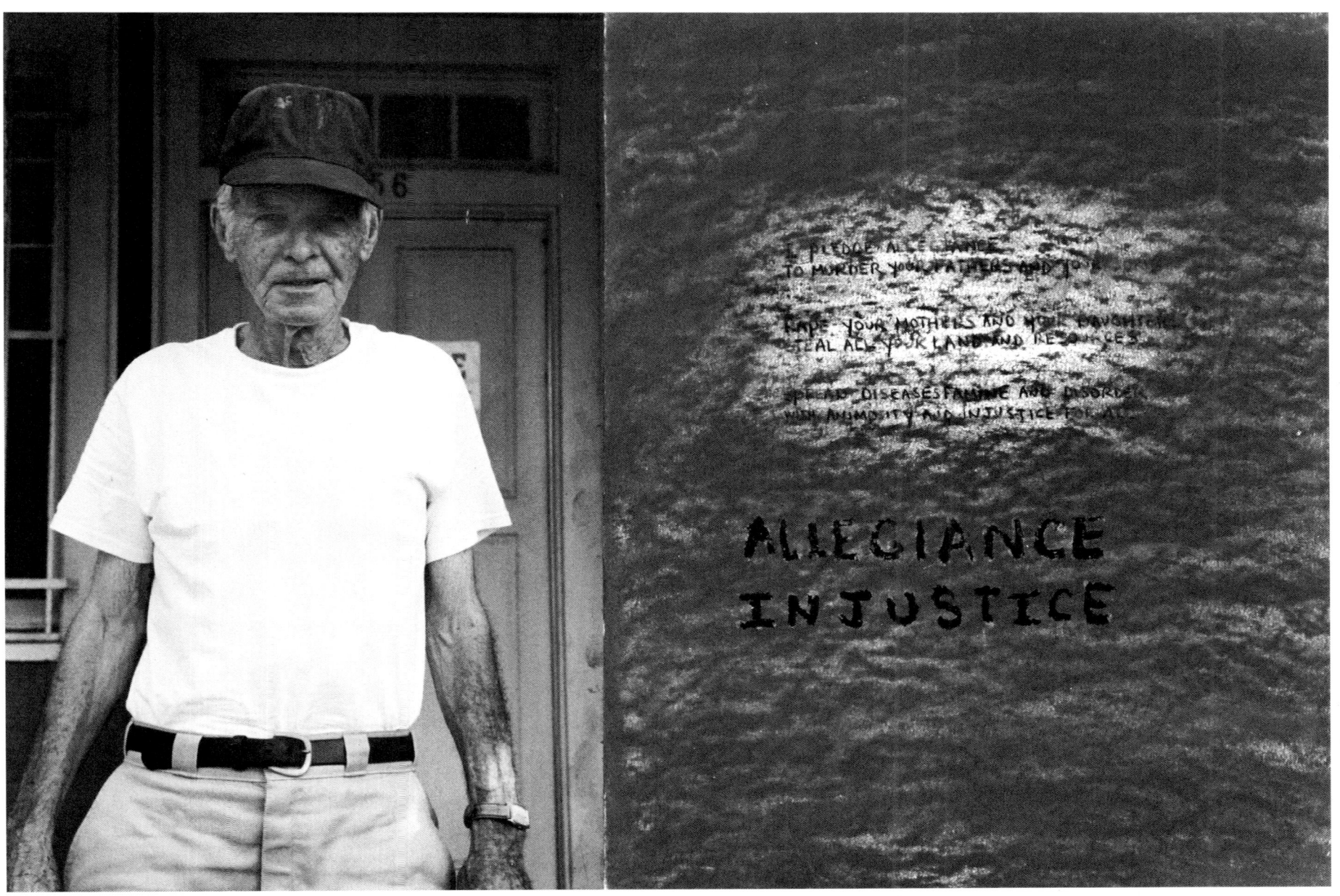

He's showing a movie he made, projecting it onto the fron

of his building.

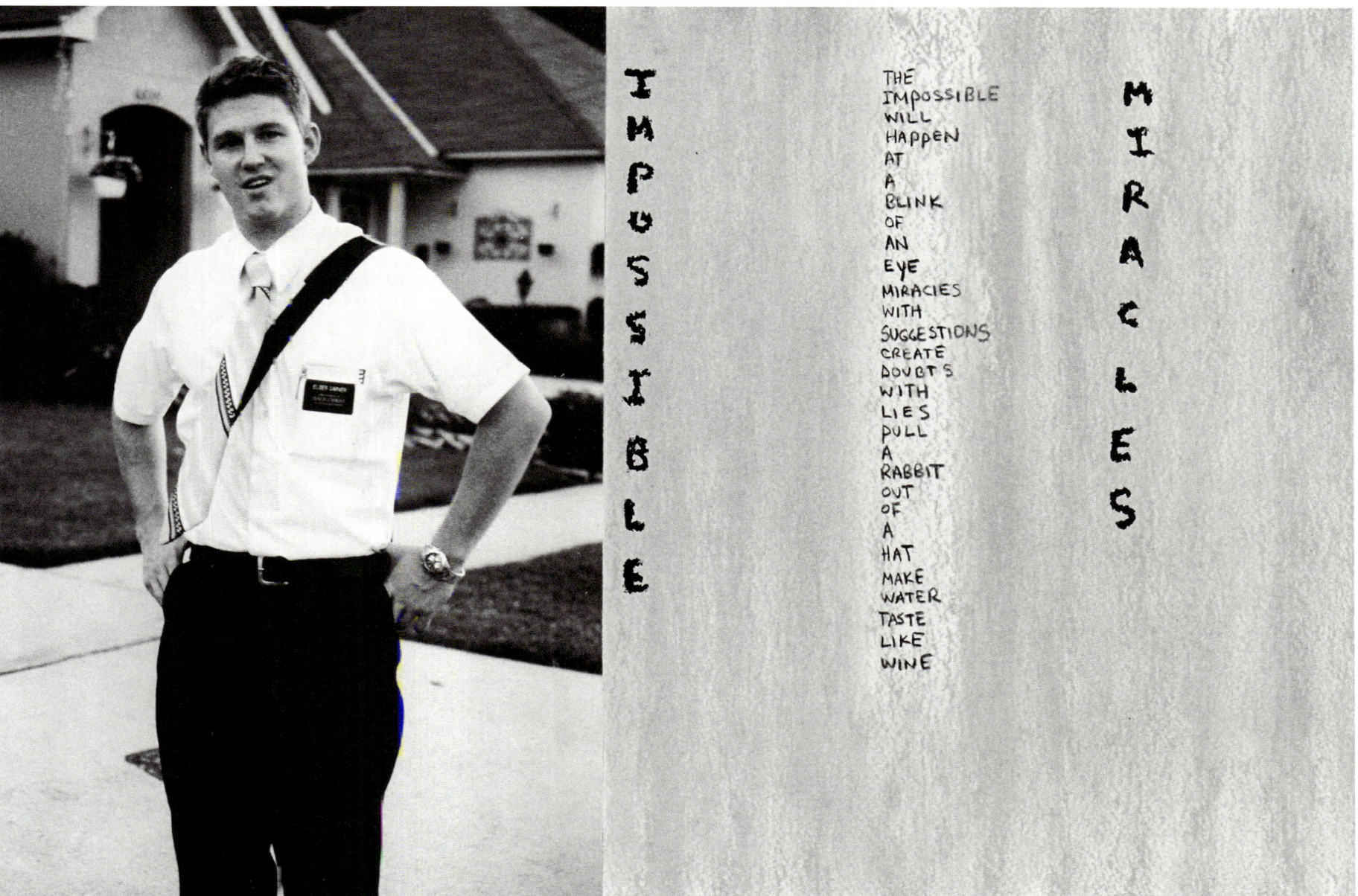

IMPOSSIBLE

MIRACLES

THE
IMPOSSIBLE
WILL
HAPPEN
AT
A
BLINK
OF
AN
EYE
MIRACLES
WITH
SUGGESTIONS
CREATE
DOUBTS
WITH
LIES
PULL
A
RABBIT
OUT
OF
A
HAT
MAKE
WATER
TASTE
LIKE
WINE

and I will always remember stopping there to talk

to a stranger and feeling better.

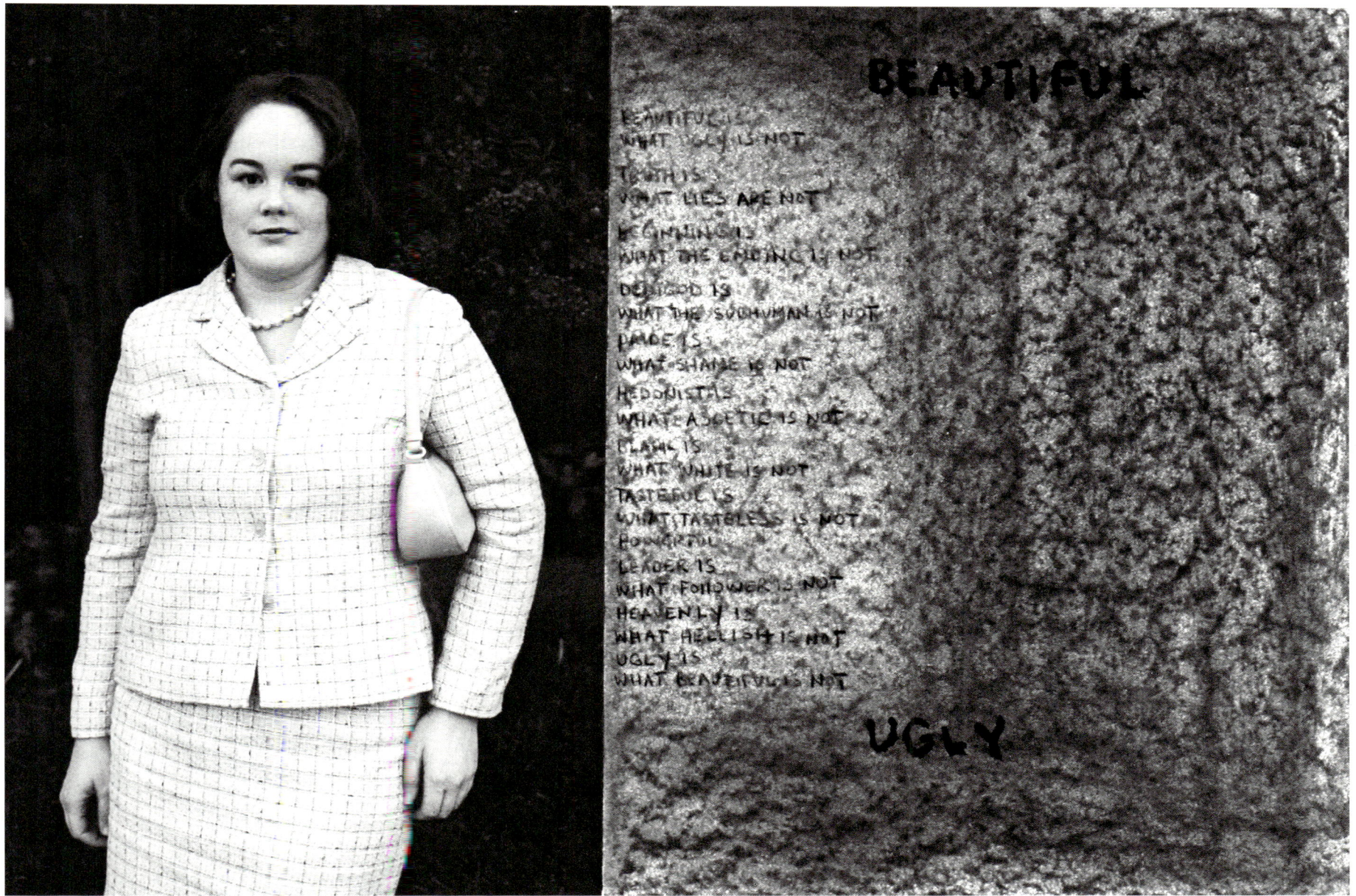

Every time I drive by that building now I remember what amounts to the strangest day of my life so far,

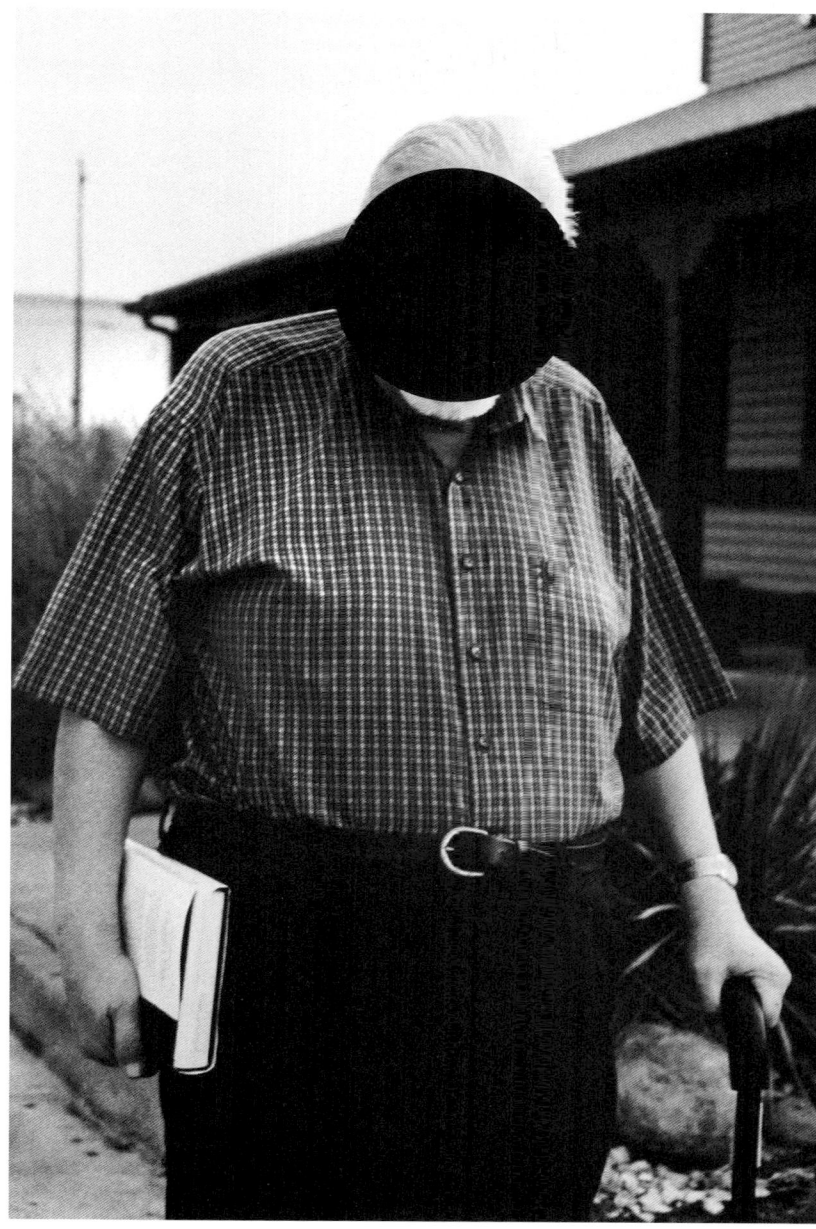

TO WANT IN THE WORST WAY
TO SATISFY PRIMITIVE NEEDS
THIS A PLEASURE
I WANT TO RAPE YOU

SATISFY PRIMITIVE NEEDS
I CAN SEE THE FEAR IN YOUR EYES
NOTHING CAN REPRESS THE BEAST
MY HUNGER HAS AWAKEN TO FEED

I CAN SEE THE FEAR IN YOUR EYES
MY ADDORATION IS DECIEVING
I'LL WAIT AND STALK YOU
YOU'LL NEVER SEE COMING
                    ME

MY ADDORATION IS DECIEVING
THEN I'LL ATTACK YOU
FIGHT ME AND I'LL KILL YOU
JUST GIVE INTO DEFEAT

THEN I'LL ATTACK YOU
CRIMES BEING COMMITTED
NOT AGAINST NATURE WOMAN
BUT AGAINST WOMAN NATURE

CRIMES BEING COMMITTED
AGAINST WOMAN BY MAN
AS YOU BEGIN YOUR DESCENT
TO THE POINT OF NO RETURN

AGAINST WOMAN BY MAN
YOU ASK YOURSELF WHY ME
WHY NOT HER
I SMELL THE SCENT OF YOUR FEAR

YOU ASK YOURSELF WHY ME
NO REASON JUST BECAUSE
THE THRILL OF THE HUNT
OPPORTUNITY PRESENTS

NO REASON JUST BECAUSE
~~CRIMES BEING COMMITTED~~
SATISFY THE URGE
THE HUNGRY WILL FEAST
AS YOU CURSE YOUR GOD

SATISFY THE URGE
THE PRIMITIVE WILL
AS YOU CURSE YOUR GOD
TO WANT IN THE WORST WAY

WANT

PRIMITIVE

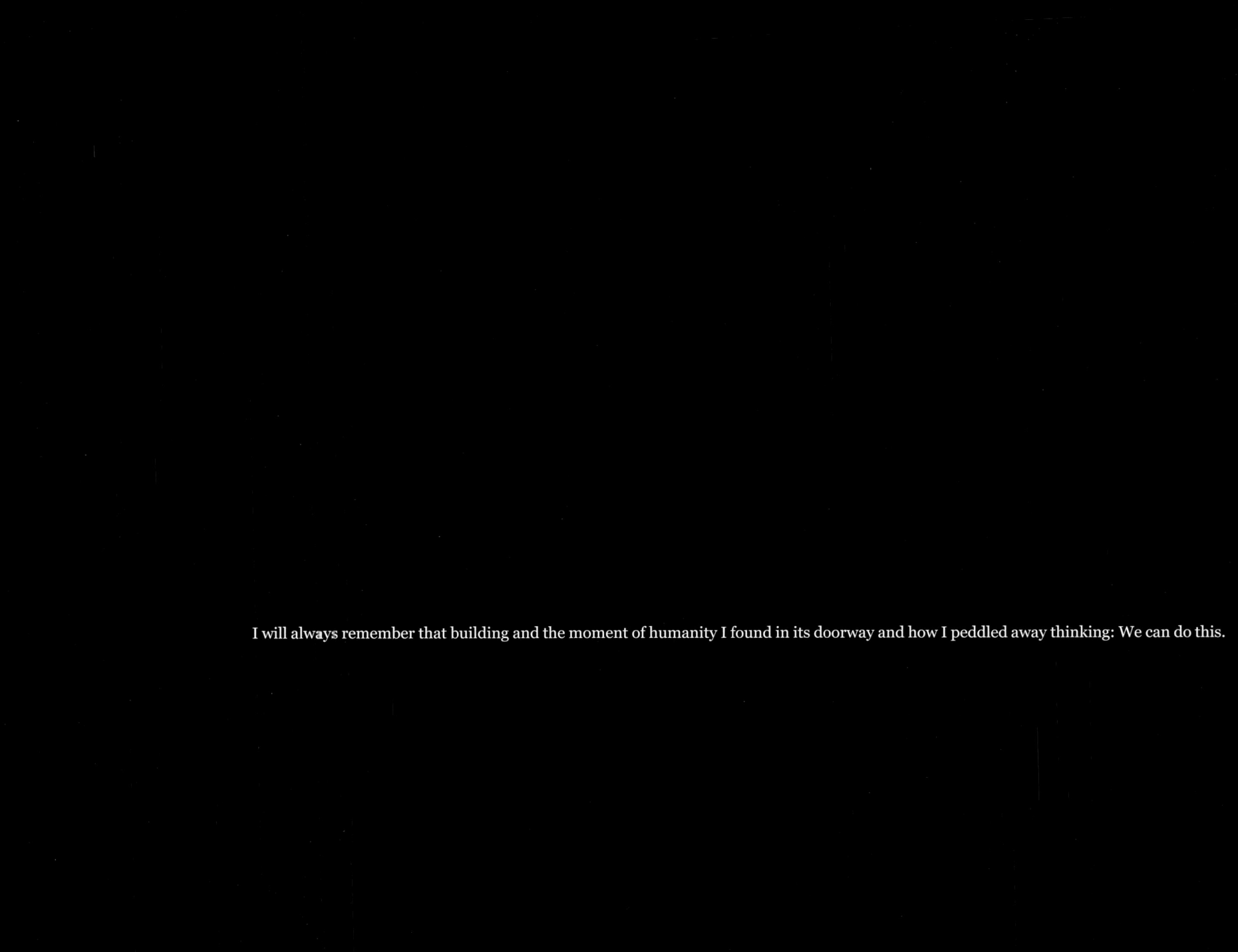

I will always remember that building and the moment of humanity I found in its doorway and how I peddled away thinking: We can do this.

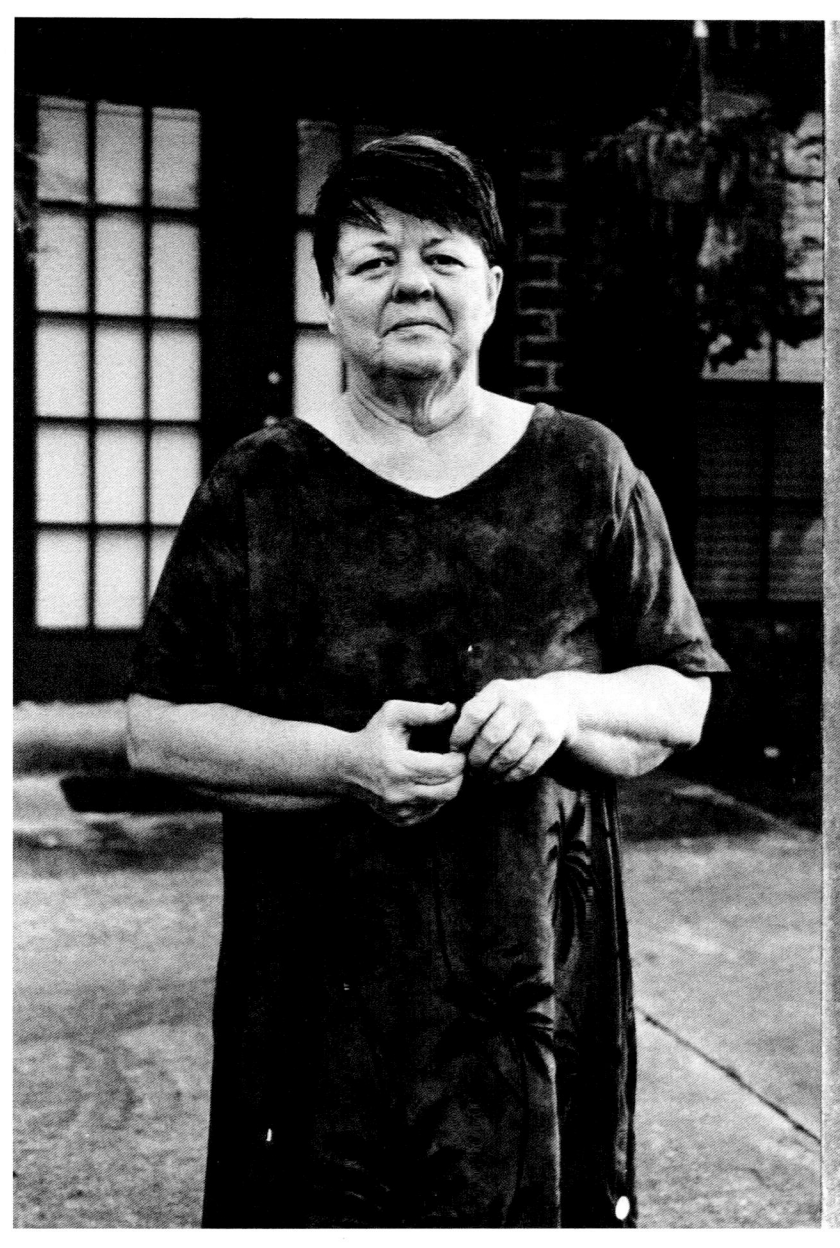

FEAR OF LIVING

AFRAID TO QUESTION

PERSECUTION AND TREASON

ORIGINS of beginnings

FACTS ARE MISLEADING

FORCED SINCE BIRTH

FOR SPIRITUAL SLAVERY

AND TEN PERCENT OF YOUR INCOME

ORIGIN

I want to thank, Oak Porcelli, Melissa Dizon (EBirth) Meline Dizon Anne Dizon, JoJo, Marianne, Eleanor, Julius, Ann, Marilyn, Grandma, Willie Horton Humble, John Stone, Olivia Hill, Tony Notero, Sedona Lincoln, Dan Cameron Shinelle Lewis, Layla Messaoub, Stephen Collins, Luke, Clint, Robin Arnold, Simon, Helen, Sally, Julie Gasgont, Brett Brent, Jessica, Ryan (one eyed Jacks) Michael Wiszniak, "R" Bam, St. Ives Pete, Dave Banks, Stan Sellon, Mitch Horteman Chad Anderson, Mimi, Christie Blodney, Yuki, Tahanna, Carolyn Somers, Moussa Sentore, Chris Gonzalez, Chris Moze, Doug MacCash, Erik Bookhardt, Guernie Art Solvers, KK projects, Kirsha Kaechele, Vyonya Tserenbaljid, Kyaw Bishop, Kristin Capps, Jenelle Davis, Irene Berningenbon. Amanda Lash Jim Mulvhill, Arthur Nagos, Timothy Vermut, Steven McCleely, Ivy Gladden Jennifer (Michelangelo), Ann Home Popko, Tara, Jessie, Kikala, Mario Moluo, Bruce Keyes, Sherm, Blake + Zach. Dudy Const, Leslie, Denise, Christy, Robert Tannen, Willye Bush, Ron Becht, Danielle, Grusec Ken Capone, Jennifer Pagan, Michelle Elmore, Owen Murphy, Bryce, Simon Hunter. Meghan Duthy, Marin + Ariel, Ariel Jackson, Sanford Biggers, Patrick Finney, Bruce Davenport, Z. Tina Giblin, Keith Neeguaye, Sigmund, Tony Deplint

DAY 3   It was so dark at night pitch black

My Son William,

I never imagined the tenderness of stars watch you drain out.   There were

I remember being —

Superdome was A Disney a typhoon of

Helicopters were right over my roof

VIRGIN was Also going Katrina   DAY 2   He could suffer on   city out of   white bricks

Ironic that seems the bombardment   have done anything   break that worked.

DAY 7 — Tfertibly from the of send the   child with police sirens on

Who's to blame   I saw her w/ three children   hottest   fight to take the city   took   DAY 11   Black white ones

— My helicopter stayed on the entire time   all over the country   I listed   DAY 1   mud was bad everywhere   in

Red Cross And   There were police sirens   DAY 7   Army   to reopen   My furnish   there now   I never saw Flight

Salvation   also right now   occupied   Hi Kato   I list with   must A fuel fu

Another gun Asked me who   A CARAVAN in A   I list with   the dust   stay what.

DAY 6   ?   honorable store.   Lit' Baghdad   T-shirts

Knowowne was I stove the   there was   ?   we all are   Day 4

DAY 10   police pushy cold furn airport   like the new feels   the sun was shy it was a

— It was   stay same.   76   beautiful day.   What Are you still doing   DAY 8

the

This atrocity was one of the saddest I ever city

witnessed.   Day 9   You better get out while you can

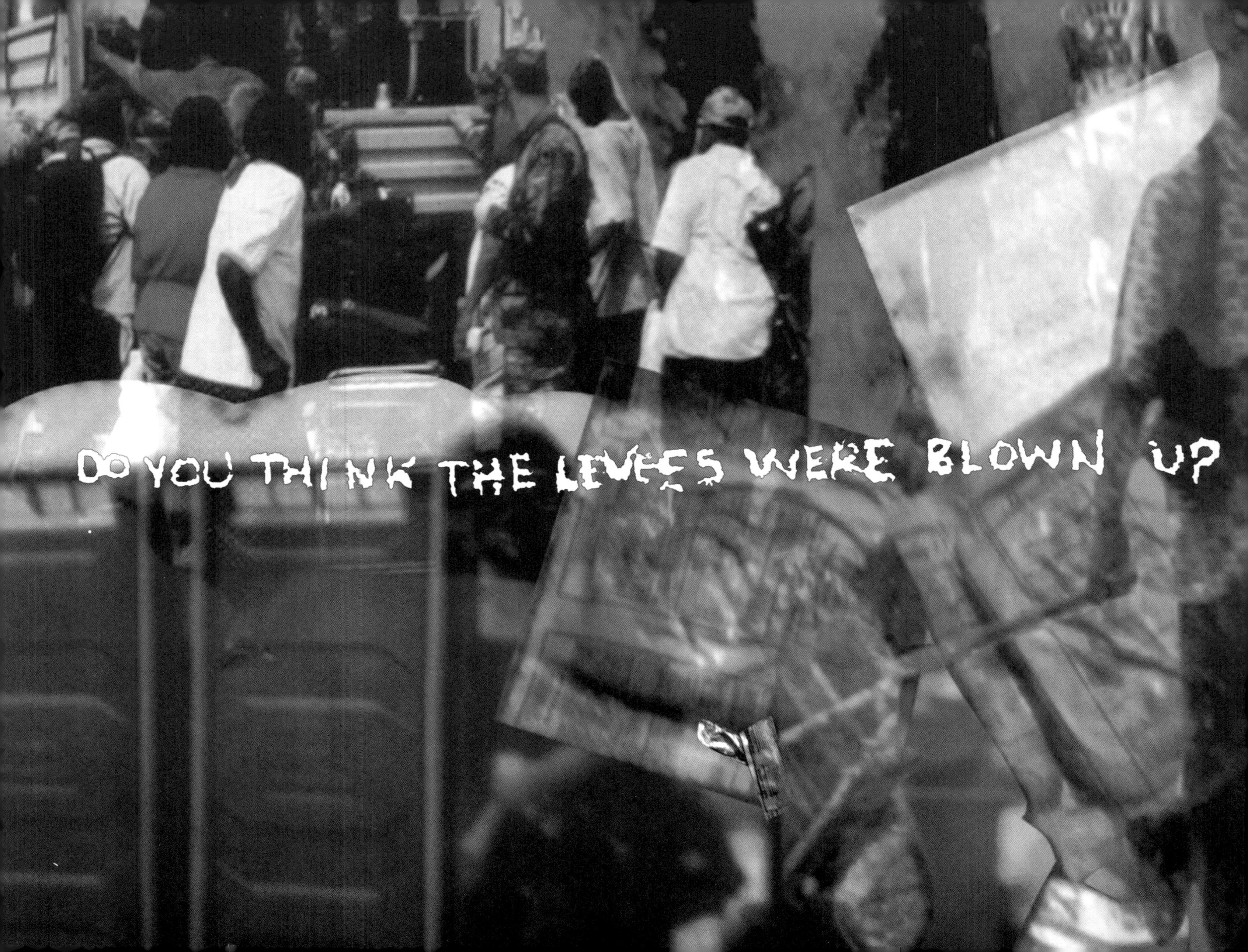
DO YOU THINK THE LEVEES WERE BLOWN UP?

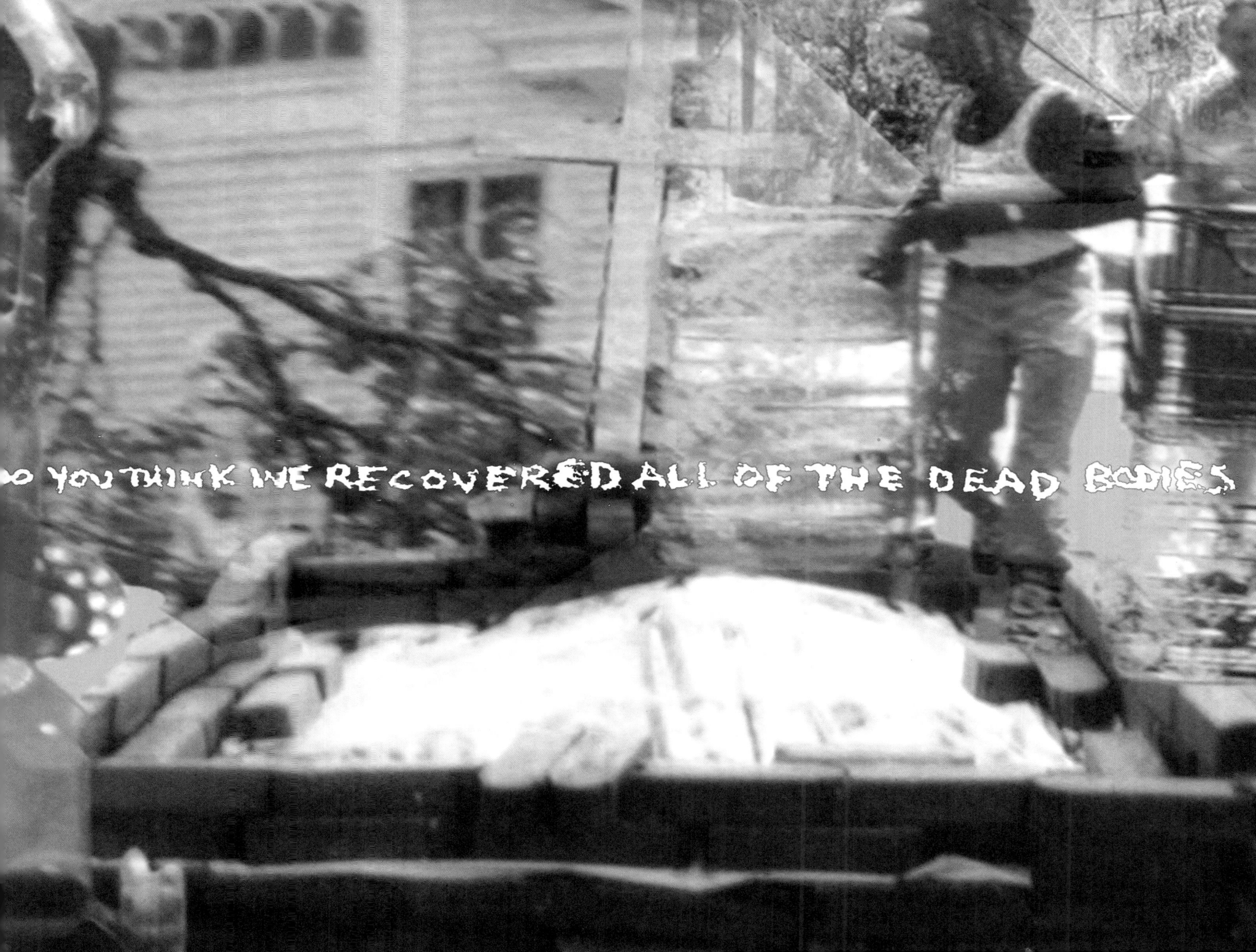

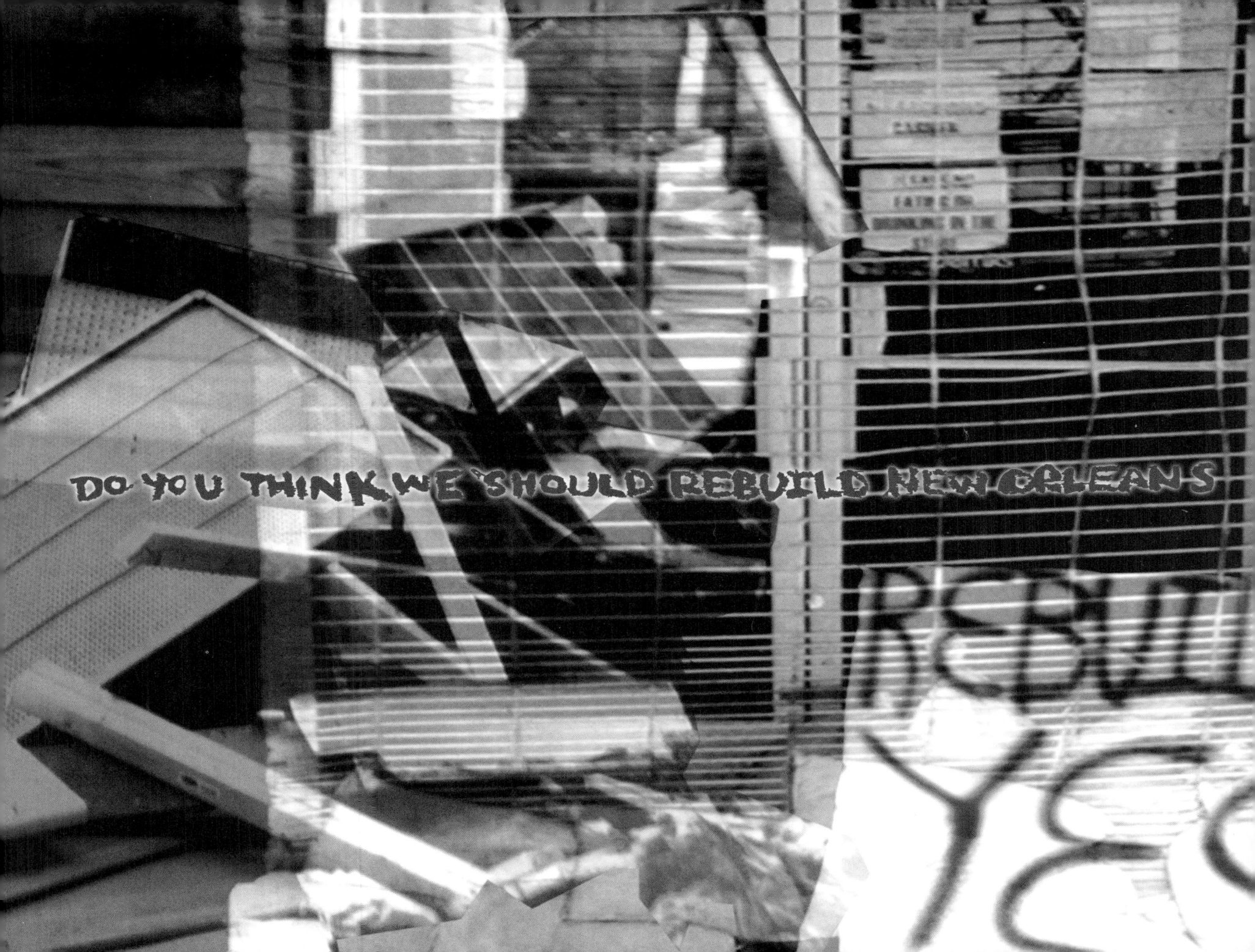

DO YOU THINK POST KATRINA NEW ORLEANS IS SAFER

DO YOU THINK RACE RELATIONS HAVE IMPROVED POST KATRINA

DO YOU THINK PEOPLE ARE SICK OF TALKING ABOUT KATRINA

DO YOU THINK NEW ORLEANS IS LESS CORRUPT POST KATRINA

DO YOU THINK NEW ORLEANS PROFITED FROM KATRINA

Miranda Lash,

Curator of Modern and Contemporary Art
New Orleans Museum of Art,

The essential function of a memorial is to preserve a memory. Against the erosion of time, memorials resist the human flaws of forgetfulness and apathy. When executing his "Dead, Lost, or Displaced" series in the days immediately following Katrina, Sanders was unaware that he was creating his own kind of memorial. Two memories are simultaneously preserved: photographic documentation of living or once living New Orleanians. Their presence exists as an affirmation of what was and what continues to persist. The other memory preserved is one that many can relate to: the surge of emotions and concerns at that moment of crisis. The words commemorate something more intangible, but which nonetheless has a equally 'felt' presence in this town. "

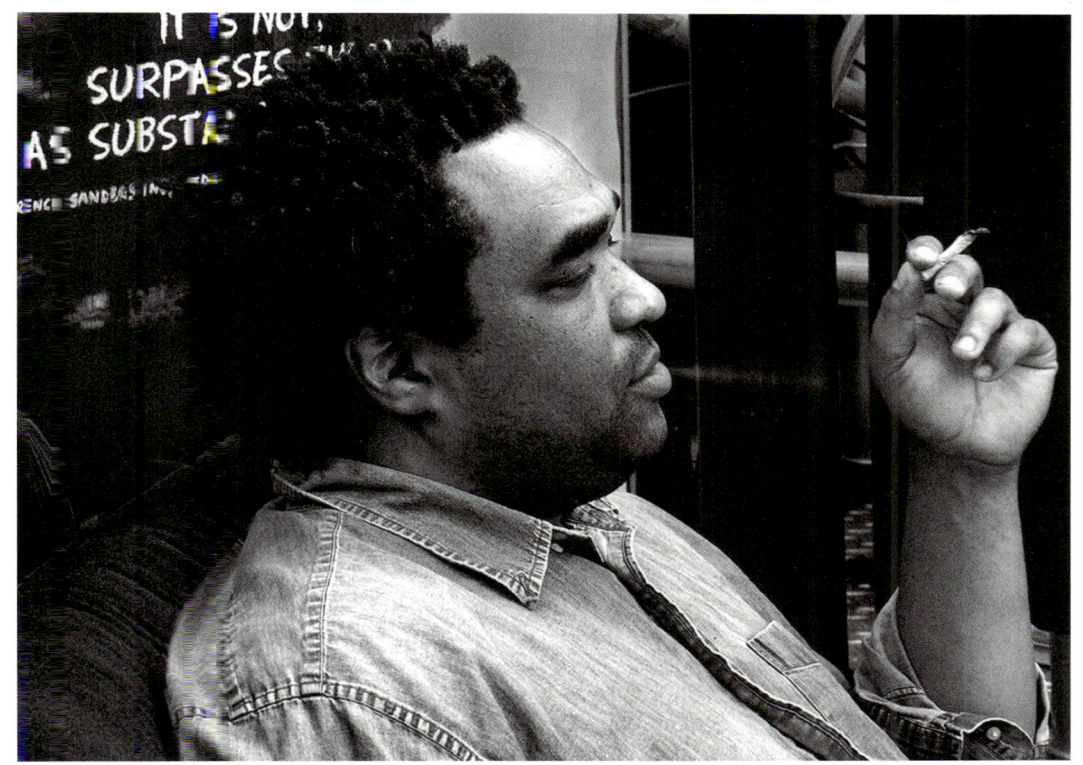

photo by Stewart Harvey

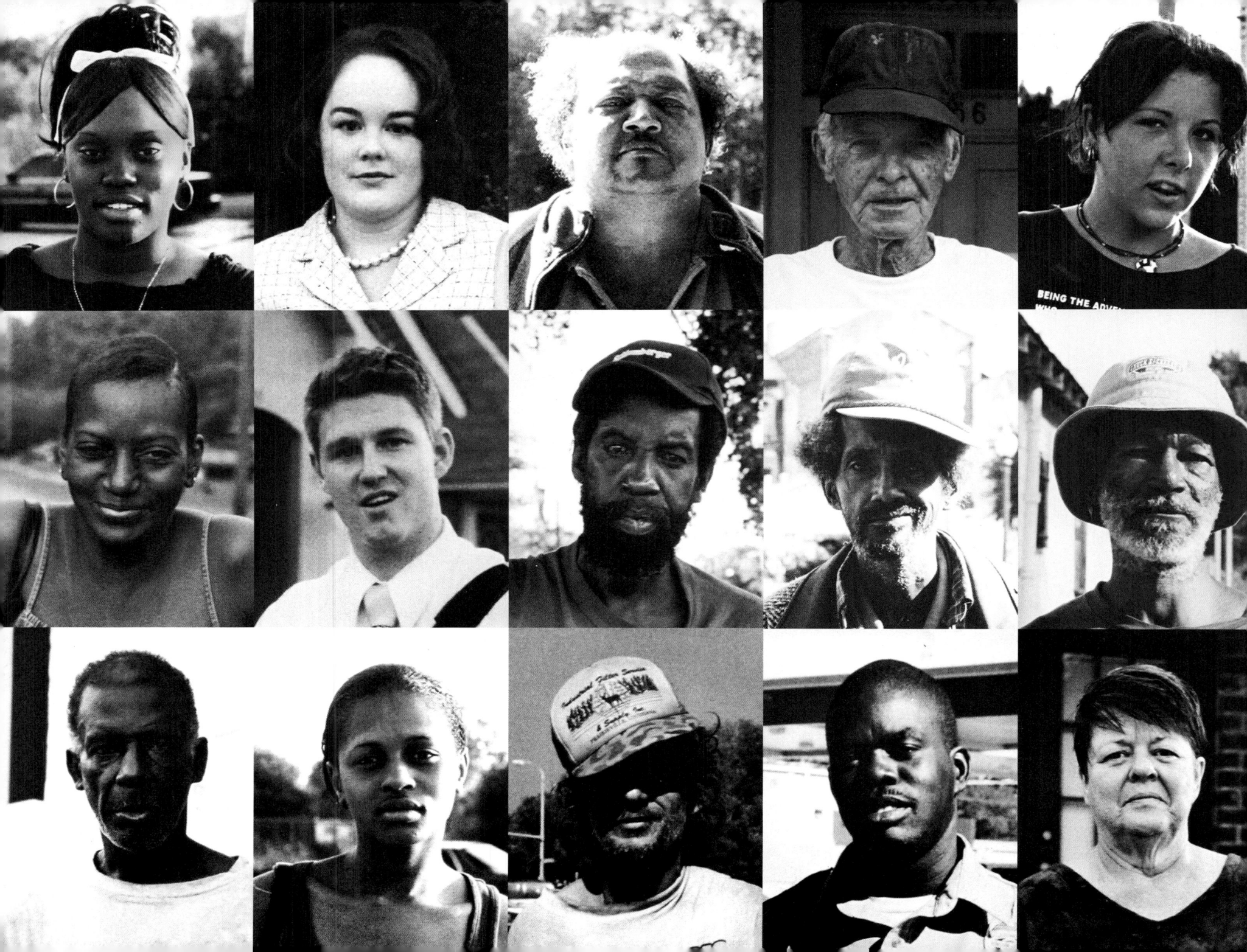